Foreign
Trade
Correspondence

职业教育经济管理类『十四五』系列教材

主编 张晚冰 李义伦 高颖欣

外贸英语函电

中国·武汉

图书在版编目(CIP)数据

外贸英语函电/张晚冰,李义伦,高颖欣主编.—武汉:华中科技大学出版社,2023.9
ISBN 978-7-5680-9902-8

Ⅰ.①外… Ⅱ.①张… ②李… ③高… Ⅲ.①对外贸易-英语-电报信函-写作 Ⅳ.①F75

中国国家版本馆 CIP 数据核字(2023)第 145438 号

外贸英语函电 张晚冰 李义伦 高颖欣 主编
Waimao Yingyu Handian

策划编辑：聂亚文	
责任编辑：姜雯霏	
封面设计：孢　子	
责任监印：朱　玢	
出版发行：华中科技大学出版社(中国·武汉)	电话：(027)81321913
武汉市东湖新技术开发区华工科技园	邮编：430223
录　　排：武汉创易图文工作室	
印　　刷：武汉科源印刷设计有限公司	
开　　本：787mm×1092mm　1/16	
印　　张：9.75	
字　　数：256 千字	
版　　次：2023 年 9 月第 1 版第 1 次印刷	
定　　价：42.00 元	

本书若有印装质量问题，请向出版社营销中心调换
全国免费服务热线：400-6679-118　竭诚为您服务
版权所有　侵权必究

前言

"外贸英语函电"是在学生掌握英语语言能力的基础上开设的一门理论性与实践性并重的课程。该课程既要结合对外贸易业务各个环节的知识，又要训练和培养有关外贸业务环节的语言表达能力，培养学生阅读、翻译及撰写各种规范的外贸英语信函以及利用邮件进行客户营销、与客户进行沟通谈判的基本技能，是一门实践性、操作性很强的专业必修课。

《外贸英语函电》的主要内容是讲授在外贸业务的整个流程中如何利用英语函电开发客户、与客户进行国际商务谈判、与客户商谈合同执行过程中的细节问题以及处理客户索赔等。本教材针对一笔完整的外贸业务来设计内容，涵盖了从开发客户到售后服务整个外贸业务流程中所涉及的常用函电。本教材共包括五个项目，分别是外贸函电准备工作、开发客户、合同磋商与签订、合同的履行和客户服务。每个项目包括学习目标、函电范例、常用句型、课后实操等内容。函电前设置有"外贸业务指引"，函电后设置有"营销知识链接"。所有内容紧贴外贸实际业务，每篇函电写作目的明确，写作指导具体，真正做到了"教、学、做一体化"。

与其他同类教材相比，本教材具有以下特点：

1. 坚定立德树人信念，挖掘每篇函电的思政元素

在习近平新时代中国特色社会主义思想的指导下，本教材深入把握新时代高校思政课课程目标，积极践行"课堂思政，立德树人"的理念，在每个项目的"外贸业务指引"和"营销知识链接"部分融入了心怀祖国、坚守信念、诚实守信、锲而不舍等思政元素，培养学生的爱国情怀，帮助学生树立远大理想，引导学生成长为可担当民族复兴大任的时代新人。

2. 结合外贸业务流程，梳理每篇函电的地位、作用

本教材在每类函电前设置"外贸业务指引"，讲述这类函电在外贸业务流程中的地位和应该发挥的作用，方便使用教材的教师结合外贸业务来讲解函电，使教学更加有针对性，也方便使用教材的学生结合未来的工作岗位思考每一篇函电的写作，使其能够学以致用。

3. 抓住外贸函电本质，讲述每类函电的构思技巧

外贸英语函电从本质上来说是利用英语函电做外贸业务，所以这门课程的关注点应该在做外贸业务方面，而不仅仅是英语函电方面。有鉴于此，本教材在每类函电后设置"营销知识链接"，讲述这类函电的写作思路以及运用到的营销相关方法和技巧，让使用本教材的学生学会的不仅仅是一篇函电，更是通过外贸英语函电进行营销和谈判的能力。

本教材由广东行政职业学院(广东青年职业学院)的张晚冰、李义伦、高颖欣三位教师共同编写,张晚冰拟定全书编写提纲并承担全部统稿工作。本教材具体撰写分工为:项目一、项目二、项目三由张晚冰撰写;项目四、项目五由李义伦撰写;高颖欣负责课程思政内容的撰写及整本教材的校对。

本教材的编写参考了众多国际经济与贸易著作、外贸函电类著作、有关教材和知名网站资料,也借鉴了国内一些学者的研究成果,在此致以诚挚的谢意!本教材的完成和顺利出版得到了广东行政职业学院(广东青年职业学院)各级领导的大力支持,在此一并表示衷心的感谢!

由于编写时间仓促,加上编著者学识和水平有限,本教材难免存在一些疏漏、错误之处,恳请专家、学者和广大读者不吝赐教、批评指正。

编者

2023 年 8 月

目录

项目一 外贸函电准备工作 1
Project One: Overview of Foreign Trade Correspondence 1

任务一 外贸函电格式 2
Task One: Format of Foreign Trade Correspondence 2
任务二 外贸函电写作原则 12
Task Two: Writing Principles of Foreign Trade Correspondence 12

项目二 开发客户 16
Project Two: Customer Development 16

任务一 开发潜在客户 17
Task One: Developing Potential Customer 17
任务二 展会前后的联络 31
Task Two: Contacting Customer before & after Fairs 31
任务三 与客户日常沟通 39
Task Three: Daily Communication with Customer 39

项目三 合同磋商与签订 50
Project Three: Contract Negotiation and Signing 50

任务一 询盘 51
Task One: Enquiry 51
任务二 发盘 59
Task Two: Offer 59
任务三 还盘 73
Task Three: Counter-offer 73

任务四　接受与签订合同 83
　　Task Four: Acceptance and Signing Contract 83

项目四　合同的履行 89
Project Four: Execution of Contract 89

　　任务一　包装 90
　　Task One: Packing 90

　　任务二　支付 99
　　Task Two: Payment 99

　　任务三　保险 116
　　Task Three: Insurance 116

　　任务四　装运 123
　　Task Four: Shipping 123

项目五　客户服务 133
Project Five: Customer Service 133

　　任务一　索赔与理赔 134
　　Task One: Claim and Settlement 134

　　任务二　售后跟进 143
　　Task Two: After-sale Follow-up 143

参考文献 149

项目一　外贸函电准备工作

Project One: Overview of Foreign Trade Correspondence

学习目标

【思政目标】

培养学生严谨认真的业务素养；
培养学生良好的人文修养、沟通协作的业务素养；
培养学生精益求精的工匠精神。

【知识目标】

掌握外贸函电的布局、格式及各个构成部分；
了解外贸函电各个构成部分的功能及在外贸业务当中的运用；
掌握外贸函电的写作原则；
了解外贸业务中其他常见的通信方式。

【能力目标】

能够正确书写外贸函电各部分内容；
能够按照要求编辑外贸函电的格式；
能够结合外贸业务熟练运用外贸函电的各个构成部分；
能够利用写作原则对外贸函电进行点评、修改。

任务一　外贸函电格式

Task One: Format of Foreign Trade Correspondence

> **任务导入**
>
> 张爱华大学毕业后进入广州恒信照明科技有限公司（Guangzhou Hengxin Lighting Technology Co., Ltd.）工作，成了一名外贸业务员。张爱华入职后的第一件事是参加业务培训，通过培训，张爱华了解了公司的整体情况和主要产品，也明确了自己未来的各项工作任务。其中，最重要的一项任务就是通过各种方式开发客户、进行客户营销，而英语电子邮件是目前使用最频繁、最广泛的书面沟通方式。为了尽快进入工作状态，张爱华利用培训的业余时间，拿出了大学时的《外贸英语函电》教材，将英语电子邮件的写作格式和注意事项又复习了一遍。

一、电子邮件的构成要素及写作注意事项

一封完整的电子邮件包括发件人、收件人、抄送、密送、主题、附件、信头、抬头、正文、敬语、签名等构成要素，如下所示。

发件人（From）	Zhangaihua@mail.hengxin.com
收件人（To）	Johnson@yaoo.com
抄送（Cc）	salesmanager@mail.hengxin.com
密送（Bcc）	
主题（Subject）	Offer for 1,000 glowing bath toys
附件（Attachment）	An offer sheet
	Guangzhou Hengxin Lighting Technology Co., Ltd. Main Products: Bulb, Indoor Lighting, Night Light, Feather Light, Table Lamp, Decorative Light, Smart Home　　　　　信头（Letterhead）
	**
	Dear Mr. Johnson,　　　　　抬头（Salutation）

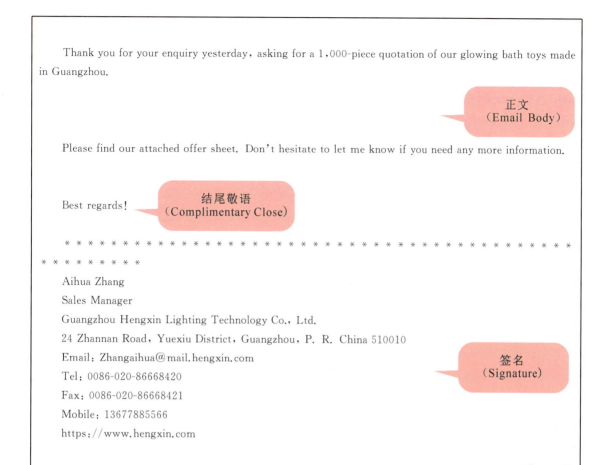

1. 发件人(From)

给客户发邮件尽量使用企业邮箱,企业邮箱是指以企业的域名作为后缀的电子邮件地址。企业邮箱具有推广企业形象、便于管理、提供专业技术服务等优点,所以很多公司会给员工分配企业邮箱账号,甚至要求员工必须使用企业邮箱来处理业务。而对于外贸业务员来说,使用企业邮箱也更容易取信于客户。

2. 收件人(To)

首先,在输入收件人电子邮件地址时,要认真细心,多检查几遍,尤其要注意字母大小写和特殊符号。如果可以,尽量用复制粘贴的方式输入,避免手动输入。其次,要善于利用邮箱提供的"群发单显"功能,即在用电子邮箱群发邮件的时候,会采用一对一发送的方式,这样每个收件人看到的都是该邮件单独发给了自己,不会显示群发,以此避免因群发而造成可能的客户不快,同时也方便了自己的工作。

3. 抄送(Cc)、密送(Bcc)

抄送的英文全称是 carbon copy,指的是将邮件同时发送给收件人以外的人,并且收件人也可以看到邮件被抄送给了其他人。抄送的目的主要分为两种。一种是知会,就是让自己的同事或者上司了解工作情况。比如在处理某项业务时,你的经理需要知道你的业务进展,那么你就可以在给客户发邮件的同时抄送给经理。另一种是寻求帮助,即希望抄送对象给自己的工作出一些主意,做一些评论。抄送相对于直接发送,约束力会小很多。抄送会给对方产生"我"可以答复也可以不答的印象。

密送的英文全称是 blind carbon copy,又称盲抄送。和抄送的唯一区别是,盲抄送能够让各个收件人只查看到邮件,而不能看到其他收件人的地址。密送可以保护各个收件人的地址,使其不被其他人轻易获得。

4. 主题(Subject)

邮件的主题很重要,客户可以通过主题快速了解邮件的核心内容,从而选择是否会打开邮件阅读详细内容。外贸函电的主题可以分为两种类型。一种是开发信的主题。开发信是写给陌生客户,希望引起客户兴趣、建立业务关系的信函。所以开发信的主题除了写明邮件的核心内容之外,还要具有一定的吸引力,促使客户打开邮件。比如,在开发信的主题中写上产品的名称和产品的优势,依靠优势来吸引客户。另一种是业务磋商及合同执行阶段的信函的主题。因为已经与客户建立了业务联系,所以此类信函的主题能够突出邮件核心内容即可。比如,如果邮件的内容是关于开立信用证的,那么就可以在主题中写上信用证的编号及"establishment of L/C"这样的字样。

5. 附件(Attachment)

应根据邮件的内容决定是否需要发送附件给客户,在发送附件时需要注意以下几点。第一,不要忘记插入附件。有的时候可能会因为粗心大意或操作失误,导致没有在邮件中插入附件,所以,在点击邮件的发送按钮之前最好再检查一遍。第二,附件应准确命名。应根据附件内容,对附件相对应的文档进行准确命名。如果以压缩包的形式发送附件,也应该对压缩包进行合适的命名,而不是直接使用电脑系统默认的命名。第三,附件不宜过大。不同国家、不同地区的网络状况不同,过大的附件可能会导致客户无法成功下载。如果确实有比较多的资料需要发送给客户,可以拆分之后分别发送。第四,注意附件中文档的版本问题。Office 文档在不同的电脑系统或不同版本的 Office 软件中显示的效果往往是不同的,甚至会出现格式错乱的问题。所以,对于一些排版精美的文档,可以同时发送 PDF 版本或图片格式的文档给客户。

6. 信头(Letterhead)

在信头部分可以插入公司的 logo,介绍公司的名称和主营业务。有信头的邮件可以显得公司正规、有实力。但信头中含有图片,可能会导致邮件进入客户的垃圾邮件。所以,是否设计信头,可根据具体情况而定。

7. 抬头(Salutation)

抬头即对客户的称呼,英语函电通常会以"Dear Mr. +姓或姓名"来称呼男性客户,以"Dear Miss/Mrs./Ms. +姓或姓名"来称呼女性客户。在写开发信时,我们往往还不知道客户的姓名,但我们应尽最大努力去获取尽可能多的客户信息,因为称呼客户的姓名可以显示出我们对客户的重视和了解。如果确实无法获知客户的姓名,称呼客户的职位可以作为次要选择,如"Dear Mr. Manager"或"Dear Ms. Manager"。如果连职位都不清楚,那就只能称呼客户为"Dear Sir"或"Dear Madam"了。

8. 正文(Email Body)

一封邮件的好坏主要取决于正文,我们将在后边的项目中详细介绍如何组织正文部分的内容,现在我们只对正文的格式提出以下几点注意事项。第一,篇幅不宜过长。业务磋商及合同执行阶段的信函可根据实际需要确定篇幅,但开发信应注意有效缩减正文字数,尽量在有限的字数内把意思表达清楚。数据表明,包含少于 100 个英文单词的正文往往会获得更高的回复率。第二,段落清晰分明。不要把所有的内容都集中在一个段落中,应根据文义对内容进行适当分段,使整封信看起来条理清晰,易于客户把握主要内容。第三,使用常用字体。尽量和客户使用一样的字体,例如客户发邮件用的字体是 Verdana,我们的回复也尽量用此字体。如果是开发信,则尽量使用常用字体,如 Arial、Calibri、Times New Roman 等。并且可以利用大小写或不同的颜色,突出重点内容。

- 请比较下列 2 封邮件的正文格式,哪一封比较好呢?

> We are a professional manufacturer of A, which has been in the field for more than 20 years. Product A produced by ourselves has got the ABC, BC, AB CERTIFICATES. As very important material in the producing process of B, our product A has so many advantages: 1. 10% power saved. 2. 10% water saved. 3. Less workers needed. 4. 10% polluted water decreased. Your destination port is C, right? Please confirm, so we can give you a current price for your check.

> We are a professional manufacturer of A, which has been in the field for more than 20 years.
>
> Product A produced by ourselves has got the ABC, BC, AB CERTIFICATES.
>
> As very important material in the producing process of B, our product A has so many advantages:
>
> 1. 10% power saved.
> 2. 10% water saved.
> 3. Less workers needed.
> 4. 10% polluted water decreased.
>
> Your destination port is C, right? Please confirm, so we can give you a current price for your check.

9. 敬语(Complimentary Close)

敬语又称结束语,它是一种客套语,类似中文书信中的"谨上""此致敬礼"等,但英文书信中的敬语往往要与信中的称呼语相呼应。其对应关系如下所示。

称呼	敬语
未知的人士	
Dear Sir/Madam,	Yours very truly, Yours faithfully,
十分尊敬、正式的关系	
Dear Mr. General Manager, Dear Mr. President,	Yours very truly, Very truly yours, Respectfully, Respectfully yours, Yours sincerely, Sincerely yours,
一般关系	
Dear Mr. Bush, Dear Mrs. Bush, Dear Miss Bush, Dear Ms. Bush,	Sincerely, Yours sincerely, Yours truly, Best regards, Best wishes, Cordially, Cordially yours,
十分亲近的商业伙伴	
Dear Mary, Hi, Mary,	Best regards, Best wishes, Regards, Kindest regards, Warm regards, All the best,

10. 签名(Signature)

签名除了写清楚自己的名字之外，还应写上自己的职位和联系方式，方便客户与我们进行商务往来和业务沟通。除此之外，还可以把公司的名称、地址、网址等信息写在签名中，方便客户一次性保存下我们所有的信息。如果把这些信息都写在正文中，一是占用了大量的篇幅，二是格式不太好编辑，尤其是地址、网址之类的信息。大部分的邮箱中都可以提前设置个性签名，每次发送邮件时，系统会自动插入签名，非常方便。

二、电子邮件的版式

一般来说，电子邮件主要有传统的缩进式、现代的齐头式以及半齐头式三种版式。对于邮件版式的选择取决于个人的喜好。如今，因为录入方便，齐头式越来越流行。它的主要特点是，信中的每一行字，包括抬头、正文、敬语、签名等，都从左边顶格开始。电子邮件的三种版式具体如下。

1. 缩进式

发件人(From)	Zhangaihua@mail.hengxin.com
收件人(To)	Johnson@yaoo.com
抄送(Cc)	salesmanager@mail.hengxin.com
密送(Bcc)	
主题(Subject)	Offer for 1,000 glowing bath toys
附件(Attachment)	An offer sheet

Guangzhou Hengxin Lighting Technology Co., Ltd.
Main Products: Bulb, Indoor Lighting, Night Light, Feather Light, Table Lamp, Decorative Light, Smart Home

****

Dear Mr. Johnson,

    Thank you for your enquiry yesterday, asking for a 1,000-piece quotation of our glowing bath toys made in Guangzhou.

    Please find our attached offer sheet. Don't hesitate to let me know if you need any more information.

    Best regards!

    Aihua Zhang
    Sales Manager
    Guangzhou Hengxin Lighting Technology Co., Ltd.
    24 Zhannan Road, Yuexiu District, Guangzhou, P. R. China 510010
    Email: Zhangaihua@mail.hengxin.com
    Tel: 0086-020-86668420
    Fax: 0086-020-86668421
    Mobile: 13677885566
    https://www.hengxin.com

2. 齐头式

发件人(From)	Zhangaihua@mail.hengxin.com
收件人(To)	Johnson@yaoo.com
抄送(Cc)	salesmanager@mail.hengxin.com
密送(Bcc)	
主题(Subject)	Offer for 1,000 glowing bath toys
附件(Attachment)	An offer sheet

Guangzhou Hengxin Lighting Technology Co., Ltd.
Main Products: Bulb, Indoor Lighting, Night Light, Feather Light, Table Lamp, Decorative Light, Smart Home

****

Dear Mr. Johnson,

Thank you for your enquiry yesterday, asking for a 1,000-piece quotation of our glowing bath toys made in Guangzhou.

Please find our attached offer sheet. Don't hesitate to let me know if you need any more information.

Best regards!

Aihua Zhang
Sales Manager
Guangzhou Hengxin Lighting Technology Co., Ltd.
24 Zhannan Road, Yuexiu District, Guangzhou, P. R. China 510010
Email: Zhangaihua@mail.hengxin.com
Tel: 0086-020-86668420
Fax: 0086-020-86668421
Mobile: 13677885566
https://www.hengxin.com

3. 半齐头式

发件人(From)	Zhangaihua@mail.hengxin.com
收件人(To)	Johnson@yaoo.com
抄送(Cc)	salesmanager@mail.hengxin.com
密送(Bcc)	
主题(Subject)	Offer for 1,000 glowing bath toys
附件(Attachment)	An offer sheet

Guangzhou Hengxin Lighting Technology Co., Ltd.
Main Products: Bulb, Indoor Lighting, Night Light, Feather Light, Table Lamp, Decorative Light, Smart Home

****

Dear Mr. Johnson,

Thank you for your enquiry yesterday, asking for a 1,000-piece quotation of our glowing bath toys made in Guangzhou.

Please find our attached offer sheet. Don't hesitate to let me know if you need any more information.

    Best regards!

    Aihua Zhang
    Sales Manager
    Guangzhou Hengxin Lighting Technology Co., Ltd.
    24 Zhannan Road, Yuexiu District, Guangzhou, P. R. China 510010
    Email: Zhangaihua@mail.hengxin.com
    Tel: 0086-020-86668420
    Fax: 0086-020-86668421
    Mobile: 13677885566
    https://www.hengxin.com

> **严谨认真**
>
> 在国际商务中,我们应该时刻坚持以严谨认真的态度撰写函电。选取合适的函电格式,并认真撰写好每一个函电构成要素的内容,包括发件人、收件人、抄送、密送、主题、附件、信头、抬头、正文、敬语、签名等。随着网络技术的发展,各种社交软件、沟通渠道的出现逐渐弱化了对函电的格式要求。但是,完整、严谨的函电格式往往会更受青睐,它一方面能够显示出我方专业的实力,另一方面能够让客户感受到我方对该业务的重视,更容易取得客户的信赖。细节决定成败!

采用合适的格式把下面的内容填写到所给的电子邮件页面框里。

(1)发邮件人。

名字:Weiguo Li

职位:Sales Manager

公司名称:Guangdong Zhongtian Lighting Equipment Co.,Ltd.

公司地址:No.9 Guangzhou Avenue,Tianhe District,Guangzhou,P.R.China

邮编:510599

电话:0086-020-22101234

传真:0086-574-22101235

手机号码:15623459867

电子邮箱:Liweiguo@mail.zhongtian.com

微信:123456Weiguo

SKYPE:v5.0.0.49888(online time:12:00 am-18:00 pm)

(2)收邮件人。

名字:Adam Green

电子邮箱:AdamGreen@yahoo.com

(3)邮件相关要素。

称呼:Dear Mr. Green

结尾敬语:Yours sincerely

主题:Thank You for Your Interest in Our Solar Lights

附件:Company Profile

邮件正文:We are delighted to learn of your interest in our solar lights. We have specialized in these areas for 14 years and we are the vendor of solar lights to Home Depot.

As you know, Home Depot is one of the most famous retailers dealing in solar powered lights. Our solar powered LED lights, solar lights, solar yellow flashing lights, solar cell phone charger, solar flashlights and solar power supply system are all included in the range of products on sale in Home Depot.

Find attached our company profile. Please do not hesitate to contact us for further information.

发件人(From)	
收件人(To)	
抄送(Cc)	
密送(Bcc)	
主题(Subject)	
附件(Attachment)	

任务二　外贸函电写作原则

Task Two: Writing Principles of Foreign Trade Correspondence

> 任务导入
>
> 在外贸英语函电的写作中，精美的格式可以给客户留下好的第一印象，但最终是否能成功获取客户，还是取决于信函的内容。目前外贸函电的写作越来越倾向于采用更加友好、简单、口语化的风格。然而，一些基本的商务原则还是应该遵循的。这些原则可以归纳为 7 个 "C"，张爱华早已将它们熟记于心，接下来就要看她是否能将之熟练地运用于工作实践当中了。

一、礼貌（Courtesy）

礼貌原则不仅仅体现在使用"please""thank you"等常规词汇上，还体现在以下几个方面：书写过程中需遵守国际商务往来惯例，尊重对方风俗习惯；回复信件要及时，即使客户的问题我们不能立即给出答案，也应及时回信告知客户已收到他的邮件，预计什么时候可以解决其问题；函电中的语言表达要客气、有分寸，避免使用命令口气，多用友好、委婉的语气。

二、体谅（Consideration）

体谅原则是指应当设身处地为收件人着想，从对方的角度来看问题，考虑对方的处境和困难，也就是能站在对方的立场全面考虑问题，理解并照顾对方的愿望、需求和感受。

比如考虑到客户与我们存在时差，需要其尽快处理的事项，应尽量在客户的工作时间发送给他。再比如，业务遇到麻烦时，应多提解决办法，少抱怨。就函电写作而言，应多用正面、肯定的表达，少用否定的表达，如下所示。

否定角度	肯定角度
You forget to transfer the money, so we can't mail your order.	We'll mail your order as soon as we receive your money.
We won't be able to send you the brochure this month.	We will send you the brochure next month.

三、完整（Completeness）

完整原则从格式方面来说，是指一封完整的外贸函电应包括任务一中讲解的电子邮件所包括的所有要素，尤其是主题、附件、签名等容易遗漏的信息。从内容方面来说，一封完整的外贸函电应涵盖所述事件的各项必要信息，如邀请信函应说明人物、时间、地点等；在回信时，对对方所提出的所有问题和要求应一一进行回应。

四、正确(Correctness)

正确原则是外贸英语函电写作中非常重要的原则。它不仅仅指单词拼写、标点符号无误、语法、结构格式正确,还应确保信函所涉及的信息、数字、事实准确无误。为避免自己一方陷入被对方发现错误后的尴尬,甚至给业务或给公司带来不必要的麻烦和影响,在函电发出前应反复审核相关信息,如:收信人的职称、姓名、地址,交货时间、地点,货物品质、颜色、尺码、单价、总价、包装等。

另外,在营销客户时应实事求是,避免夸大其词,给客户造成不专业的印象,或给后续的业务磋商及合同履行带来麻烦。如类似于"We are the largest toy manufacturer in China"或"Our products have the lowest price and the best quality"这样的表达应谨慎使用,除非有确切的证据证明你们确实是最大的、价格最低的、质量最好的,否则就不要使用这样夸张的表达方式。

五、具体(Concreteness)

具体原则是指要让外贸函电中所涉及的对象具体化、明确化。与产品相关的内容不要只使用"good""perfect"等主观词汇泛泛而谈,而应言之有物,用客观的数据和资料来说明其质量、性能、价格等;与时间、价格等相关的内容应避免类似"soon""nearly""about"等表达方式,而应写明具体的日期或金额;与单据相关的内容要写清楚编号等等。如下所示。

错误示例	正确示例
I will send the samples to you soon.	I will send the samples to you next Monday.
Your offer	Your offer No. 445 for Haier Refrigerator

六、清楚(Clarity)

清楚原则要求写信人必须清楚写信的目的,确保收信人能够完全理解写作者所要表达的意思,不会产生误解。语言表达力求清楚简练,切忌使用复杂的短语及句式。

首先,应避免使用容易引起歧义或意思含糊的词。比如"As to the steamers from Hong Kong to San Francisco, we have bimonthly direct sailings."中"bimonthly"这个词既可以表示"每月两次的",也可以表示"两月一次的",由此导致这个句子存在两种不同的含义,那么从香港到旧金山到底多长时间会有一趟直达船也就让人搞不清楚了。因此,我们在与客户沟通时应避免使用类似于"bimonthly"这样的单词,而应根据实际情况采用更加清楚的表达方式,如"We have two direct sailings every month from Hong Kong to San Francisco."或"We have a direct sailing from Hong Kong to San Francisco every two months."

其次,要正确运用英语语法,注意句子中修饰成分的位置,尤其是在修饰成分涉及时间、数量、金额等与外贸业务密切相关的交易条件时。如下所示。

	(1)	(2)
A	We shall be able to supply 12 cases of the item only.	We shall be able to supply 12 cases only of the item.
B	We sent you 4 samples yesterday of the goods which you requested in your letter of April 6th by air.	We sent you, by air, 4 samples of the goods which you requested in your letter of April 6th yesterday.

A组的第(1)句和第(2)句几乎一模一样,但仅仅是"only"这个单词的位置发生了变化,就造成了两个句子含义的极大差异。第(1)句中的"only"修饰"item",表示现在我方能提供给你方的只有这种商品,没有其他商品。第(2)句中"only"修饰"12 cases",表示现在我方能提供的这种商品的数量只有12箱。

B组的第(1)句和第(2)句中"yesterday"这一时间状语和"by air"这一方式状语的位置发生了变化,也使句子的含义发生了变化。第(1)句指的是我方寄出样品的时间是昨天,而第(2)句指的是你方发送信函的时间是昨天;第(1)句指的是你方发出信函的方式是航空快递,而第(2)句指的是我方邮寄样品的方式是航空快递。

最后,为了使意思表达得清晰明了,信函内容的编排应有逻辑性,按照不同的观点或主题进行合理的分段。信函的每段以一个话题为妥,采用篇幅较短的段落阐述,每段段首以主题句开门见山地提出每段的主要观点。段与段之间应使用过渡语衔接,如"firstly""secondly""however""moreover""in contrast"等短语,使整封信自然流畅、明白易懂。

七、简洁(Conciseness)

简洁原则是指用最少的语言表达最丰富完整的内容。在行文过程中尽量选用简单、常用、易懂、朴素的词汇,采用简洁、直接的句子,以提高沟通效率。一封拖沓冗长、措辞复杂的书信不仅写时费力,对方阅读时更浪费时间,有时甚至看不懂。故撰写外贸函电时要长话短说,避免啰唆,用尽可能少的简单的文字,完整清楚地表达出需要表达的意思即可。

首先,避免写无意义的话,如"Are you interested in our products?""Would you like to cooperate with us?"等。其次,多使用简短常用的词汇,而不选择生僻的低频词汇。最后,尽量使用简单的短句。有研究表明,7~20个单词组成的句子表达更清晰,而含有20个单词以上的句子理解起来会有困难或使人觉得厌烦。所以我们应尽量用较短的句子来表达,或将一个长句、复合句拆分成几个简单句来表达。如下所示。

错误示例	正确示例
Please see that an enquiry is conducted to determine the reason.	Please find out the reason.

错误示例	正确示例
It has been decided that due to the present situation of the company concerning a decrease in sales, coupled with the increasing cost of raw materials, radical cost savings are to be implemented by each division.	The company is facing a decrease in sales and an increase in the cost of raw materials. Therefore, each division must implement cost savings.

思政园地

1. 人文修养、沟通协作

遵循礼貌、体谅原则,以礼为先,提升人文修养,有利于在沟通协作中促成交易,弘扬我国的优良传统文化。礼貌,不仅是良好人文素质的体现,同时也是专业能力的一种标配。礼貌用语能够给客户留下良好印象,并能彰显中华民族礼仪之邦的大国风范。体谅,能够促进相互谅解、相互包容,减少误解和矛盾,使双方更好地以沟通协作精神解决问题,提高业务效率,达到互利共赢。

2. 精益求精的工匠精神

遵循完整、正确、具体、清楚、简洁原则,培养精益求精的工匠精神。无论是函电的格式、内容的组织,还是语句的表达、短语的运用、单词的拼写等等,都要仔细琢磨、力求完善。在商务函电中,只有培养执着专注、精益求精、一丝不苟、追求卓越的工匠精神,才能赢得更多客户的信任,取得更长远的发展。

课后习题

请根据 7C 写作原则将下列句子修改成更好的表达方式。

(1) Tell me your detailed requirements.

(2) You can't visit our plant this weekend.

(3) The goods you ordered couldn't be shipped on Dec. 25th, 2021.

(4) The price of our goods is the lowest.

(5) We are the most famous lighting manufacturer in China.

(6) I will send the quotation sheet to you soon.

(7) The price of this night light is about USD 10.

(8) As to the steamers from Hong Kong to San Francisco, we have bimonthly direct sailings.

项目二 开发客户

Project Two: Customer Development

学习目标

【思政目标】

培养学生的文化自信,弘扬我国的企业文化并展示中国制造、中国品牌;

培养学生的爱岗敬业精神和创新精神,引导学生养成良好的业务习惯;

培养学生的爱国主义精神,引导学生尊重文化多元,弘扬中华传统文化。

【知识目标】

掌握外贸开发信、展会后联络信函及日常沟通信函的常用英文词汇及句型;

掌握外贸开发信、展会后联络信函及日常沟通信函的内容及写作方法和技巧;

掌握分析客户的途径和方法;

掌握介绍公司和产品的技巧与方法。

【能力目标】

能够利用所学知识对不同的外贸开发信进行分析比较;

能够通过互联网查找、搜集客户信息并分析客户需求;

能够合理利用FABE法则介绍公司和产品;

能够撰写布局合理、内容具体的外贸开发信、展会后联络信函及日常沟通信函。

任务一　开发潜在客户

Task One: Developing Potential Customer

> **任务导入**
>
> 顺利完成了业务培训后，张爱华信心满满地开启了自己的外贸之旅。对于一个业务员来说，开发客户是自己要闯过去的第一个难关。张爱华通过跨境电商平台、搜索引擎、社交软件等途径搜集整理了潜在客户的信息，在分析客户需求的基础上，她开始撰写邮件推销自己的产品。张爱华一共撰写了4封外贸开发信，请大家在阅读、翻译信函的基础上，分析4封开发信的优、缺点，并总结撰写开发信的方法和技巧。

外贸业务指引

　　撰写外贸开发信是外贸业务员获取客户、寻求建立业务关系最常用的方式。外贸开发信是指向完全陌生的客户推销产品的信函，也是外贸业务中写作起来最有难度的一类信函。对于完全陌生的客户，因为没有任何的感情基础，所以完全要靠信函本身来打动客户。并且我们对客户的了解也十分有限，因而需要提前尽可能多地搜集客户信息，从而分析客户的各种需求，进行有针对性的营销。

一、外贸开发信（1）

发件人（From）	Zhangaihua@mail.hengxin.com
收件人（To）	Johnson@yaoo.com
主题（Subject）	Lights
时间（Time）	July 16th, 2021
附件（Attachment）	

Dear Mr. Johnson,

Have a nice day!

We learn from www.alibaba.com that you are in the market for lights.

This is Guangzhou Hengxin Lighting Technology Co., Ltd., specializing in the manufacture and export of lights. Our products are of excellent quality and competitive price. For more information, pls visit our website：http://www.hengxin.com.

If you need our quotations, pls send me your enquiry by email. We sincerely look forward to establishing good business relations with you.

Waiting for your kindly reply.

Best regards！

Aihua Zhang
Sales Manager
Guangzhou Hengxin Lighting Technology Co., Ltd.
24 Zhannan Road, Yuexiu District, Guangzhou, P. R. China 510010
Email：Zhangaihua@mail.hengxin.com
Tel：0086-020-86668420
Fax：0086-020-86668421
Mobile：13677885566
https://www.hengxin.com

1. 常用词汇

light	发光体,光源,(尤指)电灯
learn from	从……得知
in the market for	想要购买
lighting	照明
specialize	专门从事,(在某事物上)有专长
manufacture	(用机器)大量生产,成批制造
export	出口
competitive	(商品、服务)有竞争力的
quotation	报价
enquiry	询问,打听(专业:询盘)
establish	建立,创立,设立

2. 常用句型

(1) We learn from www.alibaba.com that you are in the market for lights.

(2) This is Guangzhou Hengxin Lighting Technology Co., Ltd., specializing in the manufacture and export of lights.

(3) Our products are of excellent quality and competitive price.

(4) We sincerely look forward to establishing good business relations with you.

(5) Waiting for your kindly reply.

• 你觉得这封开发信写得怎么样？如果你是客户，你愿意回信给张爱华，与其建立业务关系吗？

营销知识链接

从营销效果来看，这封开发信的内容过于空洞，没有介绍清楚自己的产品，更没有能够打动客户的利益点，很难让人产生购买产品的欲望。灯具包含的范围非常宽泛，你销售的具体产品究竟是什么，应在信函中明确告知客户。信函中对产品的介绍仅仅包含质量好和价格有竞争力这两项主观的描述，但何为质量好、价格是多少仍然让客户存在疑问。在没有介绍清楚任何产品信息的情况下，就让客户自己去浏览网站、了解详情，很显然是没有站在客户角度、为客户着想的，不符合函电写作的"体谅"这一原则。

二、外贸开发信(2)

发件人(From)	Zhangaihua@mail.hengxin.com
收件人(To)	Johnson@yaoo.com
主题(Subject)	Lights
时间(Time)	July 16th, 2021
附件(Attachment)	

Dear Mr. Johnson,

We got your information from www.alibaba.com. I am Aihua Zhang from Guangzhou Hengxin Lighting Technology Co., Ltd., and writing to you for the establishment of business relations.

Our company was established in 2006, specializing in manufacturing bulb, indoor lighting, night light, feather light, table lamp, decorative light, smart home, etc. We have 20 developing engineers and more than 350 skilled workers.

The workshop occupies 5,000 square meters and has an independent mold department and injection molding plant, including 4 CNC machining centers, 20 injection molding machines and 4 assembly lines. The annual output value is 13 million US dollars.

What's more, our goods enjoy fast sales in various places at home and abroad. Such as Europe, South America, North America, Mid-East, Southeast Asia and so on.

Please feel free to contact me for any question.

Yours faithfully,

Aihua Zhang
Sales Manager
Guangzhou Hengxin Lighting Technology Co., Ltd.
24 Zhannan Road，Yuexiu District，Guangzhou, P. R. China 510010
Email：Zhangaihua@mail.hengxin.com
Tel：0086-020-86668420
Fax：0086-020-86668421
Mobile：13677885566
https://www.hengxin.com

1. 常用词汇

bulb	电灯泡
indoor lighting	室内照明设备
night light	夜间照明灯,夜灯
feather light	羽毛灯
table lamp	台灯
decorative light	装饰灯
smart home	智能家居
developing engineer	研发工程师
skilled worker	熟练工人
occupy	使用,占用(空间、面积、时间等)
mold department	模具部
injection molding plant	注塑厂
CNC	数控(computer numerical control)
assembly line	装配线
annual output value	年产值
enjoy fast sales	畅销

2. 常用句型

(1) The workshop occupies 5,000 square meters.
(2) The annual output value is 13 million US dollars.
(3) What's more, our goods enjoy fast sales in various places at home and abroad.
(4) Please feel free to contact me for any question.

营销知识链接

这封开发信的内容较为详尽具体，但主要内容逻辑性不强，罗列了太多的信息，重点不突出，很难给客户留下深刻的印象。信函中提到的研发工程师和工人数量、车间占地面积及机器设备数量等等信息，乍一看与客户的购买需求好像并没有什么关系，没有直击客户所关心的利益点。公司所拥有的这些资源到底能给客户带来什么好处,才是客户真正关心的问题。整体来说,这封开发信的内容,更像是向领导汇报公司情况的报告,而不像是一封营销产品的信函。所以,应结合客户的需求,对信函的内容重新进行梳理总结,重点介绍我们能给客户提供什么产品和服务。

三、外贸开发信(3)

发件人(From)	Zhangaihua@mail.hengxin.com
收件人(To)	Johnson@yaoo.com
主题(Subject)	Lights
时间(Time)	July 16th, 2021
附件(Attachment)	

Dear Mr. Johnson,

It's Aihua Zhang from Guangzhou Hengxin Lighting Technology Co., Ltd.. Hope this letter find you well.

Glad to hear that you're in the market for lights. We specialize in this field for 16 years, with the strength of bulb, indoor lighting and night light. Kindly find our advantages below:
(1) Experienced in working with big customers. Thanks to the professional design team, we have become one of the largest light suppliers of Wal-Mart, Carrefour and ToysRus.
(2) Quick delivery time for decent orders. Because our output is above 300,000 PCS/M.
(3) Factory audited by DISNEY FAMA, GSV, ICTI and SGS.
(4) Free samples could be provided.

I will send the photos of our latest products in the other email next Monday. We will make you offers upon receipt of your detailed requirements.

We are looking forward to a great business deal.

Best regards,

Aihua Zhang
Sales Manager
Guangzhou Hengxin Lighting Technology Co., Ltd.
24 Zhannan Road, Yuexiu District, Guangzhou, P. R. China 510010
Email: Zhangaihua@mail.hengxin.com
Tel: 0086-020-86668420
Fax: 0086-020-86668421
Mobile: 13677885566
https://www.hengxin.com

1. 常用词汇

with the strength of	凭借……的力量
advantage	有利条件,有利因素,优势
experienced	有经验的,熟练的
thanks to	由于,幸亏
professional	娴熟的,训练有素的,精通业务的
supplier	供应者,供货商,供货方
Wal-Mart	沃尔玛
Carrefour	家乐福
ToysRus	玩具反斗城
delivery time	交货时间
decent order	正式订单
audit	(质量或标准的)审查,检查
sample	样品
offer	出价,报价
receipt	收到

2. 常用句型

(1) Hope this letter find you well.

(2) We specialize in this field for 16 years, with the strength of bulb, indoor lighting and night light.

(3) Kindly find our advantages below.

(4) Thanks to the professional design team, we have become one of the largest light suppliers of Wal-Mart, Carrefour and ToysRus.

(5) Quick delivery time for decent orders.

(6) Factory audited by DISNEY FAMA, GSV, ICTI and SGS.

(7) Free samples could be provided.

(8) We will make you offers upon receipt of your detailed requirements.

(9) We are looking forward to a great business deal.

营销知识链接

同样是介绍公司,与第二封信不同的是,这封信将公司的优势,即客户比较关心的问题,进行了总结梳理、分点列举,这样看起来条理清晰,便于客户快速把握信函的内容。另外,这封信重点突出,利用样板客户、发货速度、验厂报告、免费样品等好处取得客户的信任,激发客户的兴趣,促使客户回信。

拓展阅读

外贸企业进行的三个常见验厂和认证项目

验厂就是按照一定的标准对工厂进行审核或评估,一般分为人权验厂、品质验厂、反恐验厂等。中国加入WTO,并不意味着贸易壁垒的全部消失,企业验厂认证已经成为外贸出口企业的瓶颈,企业想接到订单,必须无条件接受COC验厂评估(Wal-Mart验厂、Disney验厂、Gap验厂等)或第三方公证机构的社会责任认证(SA8000、BSCI、ICTI、ETI、EICC/C-TPAT等),否则将失去现有的市场和企业的未来。接受跨国公司和第三方机构验厂,对我国的出口生产企业,尤其是纺织和服装、玩具、日用品、电子和机器密集型企业,几乎成为必须满足的条件。

1. 人权验厂

人权验厂又被称为社会责任审核、社会责任稽核、社会责任工厂评估等等。其又分为企业社会责任标准认证和客户方标准审核。这种验厂主要通过两种方式推行。

企业社会责任标准认证是指企业社会责任体系制定方授权一些中立的第三方机构对申请通过某种标准的企业是否能达到所规定的标准进行审查的活动。采购商要求中国企业通过某些国家、地区或行业的社会责任标准认证,获得资格证书,以此作为采购或下达订单的依据。这类标准主要有SA8000、ICTI(玩具行业)、EICC(电子行业)、美国的WRAP(服装鞋帽行业)、欧洲大陆地区的BSCI(所有行业)、法国的ICS(零售行业)、英国的ETI(所有行业)等。

客户标准审核是跨国公司在采购产品或下达生产订单之前,按照跨国公司制定的社会责任标准,也就是通常所说的企业行为守则,对中国企业的企业社会责任,主要是劳工标准的执行情况进行直接审查。一般来说,大中型跨国公司都有自己的企业行为守则,如沃尔玛、迪士尼、耐克、家乐福、BROWNSHOE、PAYLESS SHOESOURCE、VIEWPOINT、Macy's等欧美国家的服装、制鞋、日用品、零售业等集团公司。这种方式被称为二方审核。

这两种审核的内容都以国际劳工标准为依据,要求供货商在劳工标准和工人生活条件等方面承担规定义务。

2. 品质验厂

品质验厂又称质量验厂或生产能力评估,是指以某采购商的品质标准对工厂进行审核。其标准往往不是通用标准,这一点区别于传统的体系认证。这种验厂越来越多,也成了定制化审核的方向,其被称为定制化二方审核/供应商审核。以沃尔玛的FCCA为例,沃尔玛(Wal-Mart)新推行的FCCA全称为Factory Capability & Capacity Assessment,即工厂产量及能力评估,其目的是审核工厂的产量及质量管控能力是否符合沃尔玛的产能和质量要求。

各电商平台要求企业入驻时提供第三方公证机构出具的验厂报告,一般也是指此类型验厂报告。该类验厂又分为展示型和评估型,具体看平台需求。

初验厂时,一般是客户自己派本公司的审核员查验,但后来由于一些在国际上知名度比较高的企业的供货商多次被媒体曝光问题,企业声誉及品牌公信力大大下降,于是,后来绝大部分欧美企业会委托第三方公证机构代为查验,大家熟知的公证行有:德国莱茵TUV,南德等。

3. 反恐验厂

反恐是自美国"9·11"事件后才出现的,美国在全球范围从海、陆、空实施反恐措施。反恐验厂一般有两种,即C-TPAT和GSV。

C-TPAT:海关-商贸反恐联盟(Customs-Trade Partnership Against Terrorism,简称C-TPAT),旨在与相关业界合作建立供应链安全管理系统,以确保供应链从起点到终点的运输安全、安全信息及货况的流通,从而阻止恐怖分子的渗入。

GSV:全球安全验证(Global Security Verification,简称GSV),是一项国际商业服务体系,为全球供应链安全策略的开发和实施提供支持,涉及工厂的保安、仓库、包装、装货和出货等环节。GSV体系的使命是与全球的供应商和进口商合作,促进全球安全认证体系的开发,帮助所有成员加强安全保障和风险控制,提升供应链效率,并降低成本。

四、外贸开发信(4)

发件人(From)	Zhangaihua@mail.hengxin.com
收件人(To)	Johnson@yaoo.com
主题(Subject)	Glowing Bath Toy/CE, ROHS, BSCI Certified/ OEM & ODM
时间(Time)	July 16th, 2021
附件(Attachment)	

Dear Mr. Johnson,

I am Aihua Zhang from Guangzhou Hengxin Lighting Technology Co., Ltd.. I learn your brand from www.alibaba.com. Attracted by your design and after studying your product line & story, I find one of our popular items, glowing bath toy, is in line with your company's market positioning. The benefits of this product are as follows:

(1) More revenue for you
① Popular in Europe and do not have to worry about the sales.
② Enrich your product line and bring more customers to you.

(2) Soft and safe for baby
① Smooth edge and eco-friendly material to protect children's health.
② Made by high quality innocuous silica gel, can be the perfect infant teether.
③ CE, ROHS, BSCI and other certificates can be provided.
④ The waterproof grade is IP67.

(3) Variety of functions
① Combined with night light and toy. Warm and soft light could help babies to fall asleep.

② Emit seven colors of light to catch babies's attention, making the bath time more interesting.
③ Stimulate babies to beat the water and feel the buoyancy during shower.
④ Animal patterns, such as duck, whale, elephant and so on, guide babies to know animals.

What's more, we are source factory and OEM & ODM order is acceptable. Any further questions, please be free to inform us!

Best regards!

Aihua Zhang
Sales Manager
Guangzhou Hengxin Lighting Technology Co., Ltd.
24 Zhannan Road, Yuexiu District, Guangzhou, P. R. China 510010
Email: Zhangaihua@mail.hengxin.com
Tel: 0086-020-86668420
Fax: 0086-020-86668421
Mobile: 13677885566
https://www.hengxin.com

1. 常用词汇

glowing bath toy	发光沐浴玩具
brand	品牌
product line	产品线
item	一件商品(或物品)
market positioning	市场定位
benefit	优势,益处,成效
revenue	(公司、组织或政府的)收入
enrich	充实,使丰富,使饱含(某物)
eco-friendly	对环境无害的,环保的
innocuous	无害的,无危险的
silica gel	硅胶
infant teether	婴儿磨牙器
waterproof	不透水的,防水的,耐水的
emit	发出,射出,散发(光、热、声音等)
buoyancy	浮力
OEM (original equipment manufacturer)	原始设备制造商,贴牌加工
ODM (original design manufacturer)	原始设计制造商

2. 常用句型

(1) Attracted by your design and after studying your product line & story, I find one of

our popular items, glowing bath toy, is in line with your company's market positioning.

（2）The benefits of this product are as follows.

（3）Popular in Europe and do not have to worry about the sales.

（4）Enrich your product line and bring more customers to you.

（5）CE, ROHS, BSCI and other certificates can be provided.

（6）What's more, we are source factory and OEM & ODM order is acceptable.

营销知识链接

这封开发信首先分析了客户的经营情况，根据客户的需求推荐了一款具体的产品给客户，内容更有针对性。从格式上来说，每个观点自成一段，并且每一个句子都非常简短，阅读起来毫不费力，产品的优势一目了然，客户很轻松地就能了解到产品的具体情况。

对比以上四封开发信，可以明显看出第三封和第四封要远远好于前两封。由此可见，一封好的外贸开发信，应从内容和布局两个方面入手。

1. 外贸开发信的内容

在撰写外贸开发信之前，一定要清楚给客户写开发信的目的是什么。大家应该都很清楚，撰写开发信的目的是与客户建立业务关系，但往往很多人会忽略了建立业务关系的基础是什么。毫无疑问，客户最终之所以会愿意和我们建立业务关系，一定是因为他想要购买我们的产品，所以，开发信的核心应该是介绍产品。遗憾的是，现实当中有很多开发信，通篇看完也不知道产品究竟是什么样的，那这样的开发信肯定不能发挥其应有的作用。

另外，一封好的外贸开发信还应该是具有吸引力的，能让客户看完之后愿意回信给我们。这就要求对产品的介绍是有技巧的、迎合客户需求的，而不是只对产品进行简单描述。想要迎合客户需求，前提是了解客户的需求。所以，在撰写开发信之前应对客户进行详尽的调查，获取尽可能多的信息，用以分析客户的需求。然后，在介绍产品时，应结合客户的需求，找到产品的利益点，围绕利益点详细论述产品优势，并提供证据给客户。

 拓展阅读

FABE 法则

FABE 法则是由美国俄克拉荷马大学企业管理博士、台湾地区中兴大学商学院院长郭昆漠总结出来的。FABE 推销法是非常典型的利益推销法，而且是非常具体、可操作性很强的利益推销法。通过四个关键环节，我们能极为巧妙地处理好顾客关心的问题，从而顺利地实现产品的销售。

1. F 代表特征

F 代表特征(features)，包括产品的特质、特性等最基本功能，以及它是如何满足我们的各种需要的。我们可以从产品名称、产地、材料、工艺定位、特性等等方面去深刻挖掘这个产品的内在属性，找到差异点。特性，毫无疑问就是自己品牌所独有的。每一个产品都有其功能，否则就没有了存在的意义，这一点应是毋庸置疑的。对一个产品的常规功能，许多推销人员也都有一定的认识。但需要特别提醒的是,要深刻发掘自身产品的潜质,努力去找到竞争对手和其他推销人员忽略的、没想到的特性。当你给了顾客一个"情理之中,意料之外"的感觉时,下一步的工作就很容易展开了。

2. A 代表优点

A 代表由特征所产生的优点(advantages),即所列的商品特性究竟发挥了什么功能。我们要向顾客证明购买的理由,可与同类产品相比较,列出比较优势,或者列出这个产品独特的地方,例如:更管用、更高档、更温馨、更保险、更……

3. B 代表利益

B 代表这一优点能带给顾客的利益(benefits),即商品的优势带给顾客的好处。利益推销已成为推销的主流理念,其讲求一切以顾客利益为中心,通过强调顾客得到的利益、好处激发顾客的购买欲望。这一点实际上是右脑销售法则特别强调的,用众多的形象词语来帮助消费者虚拟体验这个产品。

4. E 代表证据

E 代表证据(evidence),包括技术报告、顾客来信、报刊文章、照片、示范等,通过现场演示、相关证明文件、品牌效应来印证刚才的一系列介绍。所有作为证据的材料都应该具有足够的客观性、权威性、可靠性和可见证性。

简单地说,FABE 法则就是在找出顾客最感兴趣的各种特征后,分析这一特征所产生的优点,进而找出这一优点能够带给顾客的利益,最后提出证据。通过这四个关键环节的销售模式,我们可以把握顾客的消费诉求,证实该产品确实能给顾客带来这些利益,极为巧妙地处理好顾客关心的问题,从而顺利实现产品的销售。

2. 外贸开发信的布局

因为是写给陌生客户的,所以外贸开发信的篇幅不宜太长,主体内容一般分为三个部分即可。

第一部分即第一段。一般在这一部分进行简单的自我介绍,告诉客户自己的名字和公司的名称及公司的主营业务即可。更多的个人及公司信息可放在信函的签名部分。如果是第一次给该客户写信,可以在自我介绍之前告知客户自己是从什么地方获知其联系方式的,打消客户疑虑。如果是老客户转介绍,就更要写清楚前因后果,以拉近与客户之间的距离。

第二部分介绍产品和公司的优势,可视情况分为若干小段,每个优势自成一段,有小标题更好。这部分为重点内容,应占整封信的大部分篇幅,但不能太长,如果优势很多,可拆分成几封开发信分别介绍。在外贸实践中,只靠一封开发信就能成交的概率很小,所以要做好给客户持续发送数封开发信的准备,因此也就没有必要一定要把所有的优势在一封信里写完。优势可从产品本身出发去写,如原材料、生产工艺、设计、包装、功能等;也可以从公司层面总结,如名声、管理、服务、样板客户、交易条件等;还可以从个人层面去写,如态度、专业性等。

第三部分即最后一段。除了常规的"Looking forward to your reply."或者"Any further questions, please be free to inform us!"等写法,建议大家在这部分写出一个实际的下一步计划,比如"May I call you by this Thursday 11 am your time?"或者"I will send the photos of our latest product in the other email next Monday."。这样既让客户了解到我们接下来的行动,感受到我们与其建立业务关系的决心,也可以激励自己坚持下去,为接下来的营销活动做好铺垫。

另外,如果邮件中有插入的附件,也可在这一部分告知客户附件的内容,提醒客户下载查看。

拓展阅读

客户为什么不理你?

在外贸实践当中,我们往往会碰到一种比较痛苦的情况,即已经给同一个客户写了好几封信,可是他从来没有任何回应,我们究竟是坚持继续写下去还是干脆放弃这个客户呢?在做决定之前,不妨先分析一下客户为什么不回信。客户不回信的原因有很多,在此列举一些常见原因,帮助大家进行进一步的分析。

(1)你找到的信息太过陈旧,这个公司已经不需要这个产品了。

分析:你从哪拿到的信息?什么时候发布的信息?

解决:能否找到对方网站,若能找到,看对方网站上是否有经营或者使用此类产品的信息;直接发邮件问客户,您是否还需要这个产品,请您告知,若您不需要,我也不会经常骚扰您,不浪费您的时间。

(2)你的收件人不是负责采购的人,没有搞清楚收件人的身份。

分析:你的收件人是采购还是销售?是中间商还是终端客户?是老板还是员工?

解决:再次调研客户,搜集更多的资料,判断客户身份,从而有针对性地营销。如实在无法获知客户的准确身份,可尝试针对不同身份分别发送几封邮件,看哪封邮件有效果。

(3)客户已经有固定的供应商,暂时并不打算更换。

分析:这一点最好有相关数据佐证,例如海关数据,或通过认识的人打听。

解决:从价格、质量、付款方式、欺诈风险、潜规则、感情因素等方面展现自己的优势。

(4)你的表现不专业,客户认为你不可信任。

分析:你是否不能及时回答客户的问题?对产品是否熟悉?报价是否不完整?对市场是否不了解?

解决:加强学习,提高自己,让自己变得专业和职业。

(5)客户暂时不需要,可能以后会需要。

分析:这种客户也不在少数,但与第一种情况不同。第一种情况是公司直接不需要了,以后也不会做或直接改行了。而这种情况是,他们还在宣传这个产品,只不过最近没有人来询价,他也就没有必要去找人问价,你的开发信或者跟踪信,他可能也暂时不会回复,因为手头上有其他的事情在做。

解决:继续跟踪。

(6)客户根本没看你的邮件,直接把你跳过。

分析:这种情况是因为你的邮件标题不突出、没新意,或者类似于某些广告,客户厌恶这些广告,直接删除。

解决:完善邮件内容,邮件标题非常重要。

思政园地

(1)坚定文化自信,维护并展示我国企业和产品的良好形象。

熟悉自身公司情况并深入了解所经营的产品,结合FABE法则,从客户需求出发,向客户展示公司良好的企业文化,向客户呈现优质的中国制造产品,推动中国企业和产品走出去。

(2)提升全面看问题的能力,知己知彼才能百战不殆。

做好市场调查,了解客户的情况,包括目标市场、需求产品、供应商情况等等,只有从客户的需求出发撰写开发信,才能更好地灵活应对和满足客户需求。

课后习题

(一)单项选择

(1)We are desirous (　　) business relations with you.
A. to establishing　　B. for establishing
C. to enter to　　D. of entering into

(2)We are a corporation,(　　) both the import and export of textiles.
A. handling in　　B. trading
C. specializing in　　D. dealing

(3)We have been importers (　　) food stuffs for many years.
A. to　　B. for　　C. of　　D. on

(4)The commodities are (　　) line with the business scope of our customers.
A. out　　B. without　　C. in　　D. outside

(5)In terms of quality, our silk piece goods are superior (　　) other brands.
A. to　　B. better　　C. for　　D. above

(6)One of our clients is (　　) the market for Chinese black tea.
A. in　　B. with　　C. at　　D. by

(7)Please refer (　　) the price list enclosed.
A. to　　B. with　　C. for　　D. on

(8)Enclosed please find the catalogues (　　) your reference.
A. to　　B. with　　C. for　　D. in

(9)Should any of the items (　　) of interest to you, please let us know.
A. is　　B. are　　C. were　　D. be

(10)Please let us have a copy of your brochure so that we may acquaint ourselves (　　) your products.
A. to　　B. with　　C. for　　D. in

(二)汉译英

(1)承蒙ABC公司经理Smith先生的介绍,我们得知了你公司的名称和地址。

(2)我们从中国国际贸易促进委员会获悉,你们有意购买电器用品。

(3)我们是一家国有公司,专门经营罐头食品出口业务,我们渴望和你们建立业务关系。

(4)我们是优质棉布与人造丝业务的主要出口商之一,由于有五十年的业务经验,我们享有极佳的声誉。

(5)我们将会航空邮寄样品一份。

(三)选择填空

(1)We are happy to learn that you, as an exporter of (　　), are willing to (　　) with us. This happens to (　　) our desire.

At present, we are interested in intelligence toys in (　　) ranges and shall be pleased if you will kindly send us the (　　) and all necessary information.

Meanwhile, please give us your lowest quotation, CIF Auckland, including our 3% commission.

Looking forward to a speedy reply.

A. medium price

B. establish business relations

C. samples

D. intelligence toys

E. coincide with

(2)We have (　　) the Commercial Counselor's Office of your embassy in Beijing that you are one of the leading rice importers in Britain. We are glad that you are (　　) China's different kinds of rice. So, we are willing to (　　) with you. (　　) please find our latest catalogue and export price list.

We are the biggest rice trader and the sole rice exporter in China. We export all kinds of rice to many Asian countries.

We (　　) receiving your enquiry at an early date.

A. establish business relations

B. learned from

C. look forward to

D. interested in

E. Attached

(四)实训操作

4~5名同学为一组,其中1名同学扮演进口商,其他同学扮演出口商。

扮演进口商的同学在速卖通、亚马逊、虾皮等跨境电商平台寻找一家企业作为自己的公司,并将公司网址及相关资料发给扮演出口商的同学。

扮演出口商的同学在阿里巴巴国际站上寻找一家销售相关产品的企业作为自己的公司,在公司网站上选择一款合适的产品,总结其优势,并分析客户的需求,分别撰写开发信给客户。

扮演进口商的同学选出写得最好的一封开发信并说明原因。

任务二　展会前后的联络

Task Two: Contacting Customer before & after Fairs

任务导入

2021年10月15日，张爱华迎来了入职以后的第一个广交会，她积极争取到了参加广交会的机会。展会前，张爱华进行了精心的准备，并给每一个客户发送了展会邀请函。在展会上，张爱华不仅对本公司的业务及本行业的发展有了更加深入的了解，还积累了很多推销产品、进行客户营销的经验。值得高兴的是，在展会期间，张爱华签订了一个订单，尽管单子不大，但极大地增强了她的信心。展会结束后，拿着展会上收集到的厚厚一摞名片，张爱华开始给尚未成交的客户写跟进信函，希望借助广交会的影响，再成功拿下几个订单。

外贸业务指引

一旦决定参加某个展会，应该在第一时间通知现有和潜在的所有客户，争取见面的机会。尤其在一些大的综合性展会和国内外的行业展中，都有可能与现有客户或潜在客户见面，获得新的合作机会。一般情况下，需要在半个月前就提前通知客户，然后三天前再提醒一次，以免客户遗忘或者没有找到相关邮件。

一、展会邀请函

发件人（From）	Zhangaihua@mail.hengxin.com
收件人（To）	Smith@yaoo.com
主题（Subject）	130th Canton Fair/ Booth No. 5H-E68/ Oct. 15th to Oct. 19th
时间（Time）	Sep. 30th, 2021
附件（Attachment）	

Dear Mr. Smith,

Glad to inform you that we will attend the Canton Fair from Oct. 15th to Oct. 19th. Our booth No. 5H-E68 will feature new night lights and feather lights. This is unlike any show we have ever done, and the new seasonal products for 2022 will surely bring you new business opportunities.

We believe that our meeting at the Canton Fair will enable you to have a more thorough knowledge about our products and lead to the further development of our business relations. We would appreciate it if you could confirm your participation as soon as possible so that we can make the necessary preparations.

Hope to meet you then.

Best regards!

Aihua Zhang
Sales Manager
Guangzhou Hengxin Lighting Technology Co., Ltd.
24 Zhannan Road，Yuexiu District，Guangzhou，P. R. China 510010
Email：Zhangaihua@mail.hengxin.com
Tel：0086-020-86668420
Fax：0086-020-86668421
Mobile：13677885566
https://www.hengxin.com

1. 常用词汇

Canton Fair	广交会
booth	摊位，展位
inform	通知，告知
attend	出席，参加
feature	（展览会等）以……为重点
new seasonal products	当季新品
business opportunity	商机
thorough	彻底的，完全的，深入的，细致的
knowledge	知晓，知悉，了解
appreciate	感激
participation	参加，参与
preparation	准备工作

2. 常用句型

(1) Glad to inform you that we will attend the Canton Fair from Oct. 15th to Oct. 19th.

(2) Our booth No. 5H-E68 will feature new night lights and feather lights.

(3) This is unlike any show we have ever done，and the new seasonal products for 2022 will surely bring you new business opportunities.

(4) We would appreciate it if you could confirm your participation as soon as possible so that we can make the necessary preparations.

(5) Hope to meet you then.

营销知识链接

展会邀请函应写清楚展会的名称、时间和地点,以及公司的展位号,同时可对展会上要展出的产品向客户进行简单介绍。

拓展阅读

备战广交会

中国进出口商品交易会(China Import and Export Fair),又称广交会,创办于1957年春季,每年春(4月15—5月5日)秋(10月15—11月4日)两季在广州举办,是中国历史最长、规模最大、商品最全、采购商最多且来源最广、成交效果最好的综合性国际贸易盛会,被誉为中国第一展。

每届广交会分三期举行,每期都有不同的参展范围。

第1期:家用电器,电子消费品及信息产品,工业自动化及智能制造,加工机械设备,动力、电力设备,通用机械及机械基础件,工程机械,农业机械,新材料及化工产品,新能源汽车及智慧出行,车辆,汽车配件,摩托车,自行车,照明产品,电子电气产品,新能源,五金,工具,进口展。

第2期:日用陶瓷,餐厨用具,家居用品,玻璃工艺品,家居装饰品,园林用品,节日用品,礼品及赠品,钟表眼镜,工艺陶瓷,编织及藤铁工艺品,建筑及装饰材料,卫浴设备,家具,铁石装饰品及户外水疗设施,进口展。

第3期:玩具,孕婴童用品,童装,男女装,内衣,运动服及休闲服,裘革皮羽绒及制品,服装饰物及配件,纺织原料面料,鞋,箱包,家用纺织品,地毯及挂毯,办公文具,医药保健品及医疗器械,食品,体育及旅游休闲用品,个人护理用具,浴室用品,宠物用品,乡村振兴特色产品,进口展。

想要在展会上有所收获,在参展前必须做好充分的准备。

(1)提前告知客户参展信息。对于普通客户可以通过电子邮件发送邀请函;对于重要客户可通过快递发邀请函,告知你的参展信息,如展位号、参展新产品等。同时可利用搜索引擎广告、社交媒体或其他平台推广参展信息,在通知到老客户的同时还能吸引一些新客户慕名前来。

(2)准备投影仪,用来播放公司宣传片,吸引客户的注意力。

(3)储备知识,包括产品知识、报价技巧、专业英语词汇和表达等。

(4)手机上预装名片管理类的 App 以及社交软件,如 WhatsApp、Viber、Kakao Talk、LINE、Facebook 等,便于与客户联系。

(5)准备必要的文具,如水笔、计算器、记录本、订书机等。其中,记录本用来详细记录客户的不同要求,订书机用来装订客户的名片。

(6)相机,用来给客户拍照,或与客户合影,可以帮助自己记忆,也可以把照片发给客户,加深客户的印象,帮助客户回忆起当时的谈话内容。另外,在不忙的时候可以去别的同行业或相关行业的展位上多拍些照片,帮助你深入了解产品。

(7)着装得体、职业化。

(8)准备小礼品。制作一批带有公司 logo 的、有中国特色的小礼品。

(9)准备一些个性化的资料,其上有你的照片、联系方式和样本上没有的信息,以及自己录制并出镜的公司宣传视频等。

外贸业务指引

除了网络资源外,各种交易会、展览会也是外贸业务员获取客户信息的很好的途径。与在网上获取客户不同的是,交易会给我们创造了难得的与客户面对面的机会。所以,我们应把握好这一时机,尽可能在展会期间多与客户接触,从而想办法签下订单。对于没有营销成功的客户,在展会结束后,趁其可能对我们还有印象,应及时写信进行跟进。

二、展会后跟进信函(1)

发件人(From)	Zhangaihua@mail.hengxin.com
收件人(To)	Albert@yaoo.com
主题(Subject)	130th Canton Fair/Lights
时间(Time)	Nov. 5th, 2021
附件(Attachment)	photos of you, catalogue of hot items

Dear Mr. Albert,

It's very nice to meet you at the 130th Canton Fair and thank you for your visiting our booth No. 5H-E68. I'm Aihua Zhang from Guangzhou Hengxin Lighting Technology Co., Ltd., which is a professional light supplier.

Enclosed are some photos of you at our booth and the illustrated catalogue of our hot items, which I believe will remind you of our company. We should be grateful if you furnish us with details of your requirements, and our products will definitely meet your needs.

Your prompt attention to this matter will be appreciated.

Best regards!

Aihua Zhang
Sales Manager
Guangzhou Hengxin Lighting Technology Co., Ltd.
24 Zhannan Road, Yuexiu District, Guangzhou, P. R. China 510010

Email：Zhangaihua@mail.hengxin.com	
Tel：0086-020-86668420	
Fax：0086-020-86668421	
Mobile：13677885566	
https://www.hengxin.com	

1. 常用词汇

enclosed	随函附上的，附上的
illustrated	有插图的
catalogue	目录，目录簿
hot item	热销品
remind	使记起，使想起
furnish	向(某人/某事物)供应，提供
definitely	肯定，没问题，当然，确实
prompt	立即的，迅速的，及时的

2. 常用句型

（1）It's very nice to meet you at the 130th Canton Fair and thank you for your visiting our booth No. 5H-E68.

（2）Enclosed are some photos of you at our booth and the illustrated catalogue of our hot items, which I believe will remind you of our company.

（3）Your prompt attention to this matter will be appreciated.

营销知识链接

展会过后，必须第一时间跟进客户，而且要简单介绍展会上的相关信息，唤起客户的记忆。即使客户不能准确记起当时的谈判场景，也必须要给对方足够丰富的资料，引起对方的兴趣。

三、展会后跟进信函(2)

发件人(From)	Zhangaihua@mail.hengxin.com
收件人(To)	Albert@yaoo.com
主题(Subject)	130th Canton Fair/Night Lights
时间(Time)	Nov. 5th, 2021
附件(Attachment)	Quotation sheet for night lights BP030，BP048

Dear Mr. Albert,

Thank you for your interest in our products during the 130th Canton Fair. This is Aihua Zhang from Guangzhou Hengxin Lighting Technology Co., Ltd.. As requested, here I attached the quotation sheet with photos for the night lights BP030, BP048.

We would like to offer discount if you confirm the order in November. Please consider and take this advantage of good promotion.

Kindly let us know your comment by return mail.

Thanks and best regards,

Aihua Zhang
Sales Manager
Guangzhou Hengxin Lighting Technology Co., Ltd.
24 Zhannan Road, Yuexiu District, Guangzhou, P. R. China 510010
Email: Zhangaihua@mail.hengxin.com
Tel: 0086-020-86668420
Fax: 0086-020-86668421
Mobile: 13677885566
https://www.hengxin.com

1. 常用词汇

quotation sheet	报价单
attach	附上（附件）
discount	折扣
take this advantage of	借此机会，利用这个优势
promotion	促销，推广
comment	意见

2. 常用句型

(1) Thank you for your interest in our products during the 130th Canton Fair.

(2) As requested, here I attached the quotation sheet with photos for the night lights BP030, BP048.

(3) We would like to offer discount if you confirm the order in November.

(4) Please consider and take this advantage of good promotion.

营销知识链接

展会后联络的信函写得好坏与否，很大程度上取决于我们在展会上做了什么。如果仅仅只是拿到了客户的名片，却对客户的其他信息一无所知的话，那么就只能按照开发信的方式去给客户写信。如果在展会上我们与客户进行过深入的沟通，对客户的需求和特点都有一定程度的了解，并且也给客户留下了比较深刻的印象，那么展会后联络的信函就可以根据对客户的了解，结合客户的需求去写。甚至可以对客户感兴趣的产品直接报价，争取早日成交。由此可见，我们在展会上的表现，以及在展会期间做好客户相关的记录非常重要。

思政园地

（1）培养爱岗敬业的精神，养成良好的业务习惯。

熟悉展会前、展会中、展会后的相关工作事务。展会前，落实好客户名单，发送邀请邮件，并做好摊位布置的相关准备工作；展会中，以亲切友好的态度向客户展现良好的沟通能力、专业技能；展会后，要密切联系和跟踪客户。对于开发信的发送和跟踪，需要注意选择合适的送达时间。在国际商务中，需要注意不同国家的上班时间和节假日安排，尽量在上班时间向客户发送邮件，并用合理的节奏跟进客户，与客户保持良好关系。

（2）发挥创新精神，挖掘潜在的每个商机。

不要轻易放弃展会中存在的每一个商机，发挥创新精神，采用有效措施把潜在机会转变为实际交易。对于展会中没有营销成功的客户，仅靠模式化的函电内容将难以攻克，要勇于打破固有的思维模式，进一步调查客户所需，包括其产品、目标市场、供应商情况等，分析我方与其合作的有利因素，然后有针对性地通过函电与其密切联系。

课后习题

（一）单项选择

（1）We would like to extend to you an invitation （　　） your visit to the 114th Canton Fair.

A. to B. for C. of D. on

（2）It is known （　　） the No. 1 fair in China and also the best one around the world.

A. as B. by C. of D. for

（3）We are （　　） that our meeting at the Fair will be fruitful and such personal contacts will enable you to have a more thorough knowledge about our products.

A. ensure B. believe C. confident D. hope

（4）It will be highly appreciated （　　） you could confirm your visit at your earliest convenience.

A. as B. if C. even though D. since

（5）Your profession of lights （　　） me a lot during our meeting in the fair.

A. expressed B. impressed C. pressed D. satisfied

(6)(　　) are some photos of you at our booth and the illustrated catalogue of our hot items.

A. Enclosed　　　B. Closed　　　C. Enclose　　　D. Enclosing

(7)I believe the photo will remind you (　　) our company.

A. for　　　B. at　　　C. on　　　D. of

(8)In order to acquaint you with the textile we handle, we take pleasure in (　　) you to the Fair.

A. invite　　　B. invited　　　C. inviting　　　D. invites

(9)We believe your visit will enhance our mutual understanding and be beneficial (　　) our future cooperation.

A. for　　　B. at　　　C. to　　　D. of

(10)Please confirm your participation latest (　　) Oct. 20th, so that we could make necessary arrangements.

A. by　　　B. at　　　C. in　　　D. of

(二)汉译英

(1)真诚期待您参加上海的国际机器设备展。

(2)如果您能出席3月5日的展会,我们将感到十分荣幸。

(3)请于11月11日前确认能否参加。

(4)相信您已经在这次展会上看到了我们的展品,请告知您目前对哪些商品感兴趣。

(5)根据你方代表王先生在广州交易会上的要求,我们很高兴给你方寄去我公司产品的样品和一份价格单。

(三)选择填空

(1)We would like to extend to you an (　　) for your (　　) to Shanghai International Food Packaging and Processing Equipment Exhibition, during Feb. 13 to Feb. 18, 2014. A great (　　) samples newly designed by our manufacturers will be on (　　) at our stands in the fair and it would be a great pleasure to meet you there.

It will be highly appreciated if you could confirm your visit at your earliest convenience so that we could make necessary (　　).

A. visit

B. display

C. invitation

D. preparations

E. variety of

(2)How are you doing? Glad to get your (　　) from China Import and Export Fair.

This is Sally from WVC Company. We (　　) parking sensor system, and all our products are CE/FCC (　　).

(　　) the FUN MINI DVR you selected in the fair, please find details with best offer (　　).

Hope to get good news from you. Thanks!

A. approved

B. business card

C. in attachment

D. specialize in

E. Regarding

(四)实训操作

4~5名同学为一组,其中1名同学扮演进口商,其他同学扮演出口商。

扮演出口商的同学在中国进出口商品交易会(广交会)的官网上查找最近一届广交会的相关信息,结合任务一实训操作中的公司,分别撰写展会邀请函。

扮演进口商的同学选出写得最好的一封邀请函并说明原因。

任务三 与客户日常沟通

Task Three: Daily Communication with Customer

任务导入

> 把产品销售给客户,并不意味着天天都在说产品,每封信都要谈业务。适当与客户进行日常沟通,不仅有助于增进与客户之间的感情,还有可能由此发掘出意想不到的打动客户的机会。日常沟通包括节日祝福、赠送礼物、升职祝贺、生病慰问等等。还可以时常关注客户所在国家的新闻,寻找话题,与客户建立密切联系。

外贸业务指引

对于许多西方国家而言,圣诞节是一年内的头等节日,相当于中国的农历新年。由于圣诞节后就是阳历新年,很多国家会两个节日连起来放假,假期长达一周或10天左右。为了避免耽搁工作,紧急的问题需要提早在圣诞节前跟客户确认好,同时询问一下客户放假的时间,并给予节日祝福。

一、圣诞节问候信函

发件人(From)	Zhangaihua@mail.hengxin.com
收件人(To)	Jones@yaoo.com
主题(Subject)	Merry Christmas and Happy New Year
时间(Time)	Dec. 18th, 2021
附件(Attachment)	

Dear Mr. Jones,

Glad to hear that your company will be closed from Dec. 22nd, 2021 to Jan. 5th, 2022 for Christmas holiday and New Year. Please confirm your order No. ABL-OP318 before the holiday, so that we can start production early.

Thanks for your support in the past year and Merry Christmas and Happy New Year to you and your family!

Best regards!

Aihua Zhang
Sales Manager
Guangzhou Hengxin Lighting Technology Co., Ltd.
24 Zhannan Road, Yuexiu District, Guangzhou, P. R. China 510010
Email：Zhangaihua@mail.hengxin.com
Tel：0086-020-86668420
Fax：0086-020-86668421
Mobile：13677885566
https://www.hengxin.com

1. 常用词汇

Merry Christmas	圣诞快乐
closed	（尤指一段时间）停止营业，不开放

2. 常用句型

(1) Glad to hear that your company will be closed from Dec. 22nd, 2021 to Jan. 5th, 2022 for Christmas holiday and New Year.

(2) Thanks for your support in the past year and Merry Christmas and Happy New Year to you and your family!

外贸业务指引

对于一些亚洲、中东地区的客户以及欧美地区的犹太人客户，需了解他们不过圣诞节，我们单独发送新年祝福就可以了。所以，对于圣诞祝福，在发送之前一定要弄清楚客户是否过圣诞节，若是画蛇添足就尴尬了。另外，如果我们自己也休假，要同时在信函中告知客户自己的休假时间，以及如果有紧急情况如何联系到自己。

二、新年问候信函

发件人(From)	Zhangaihua@mail.hengxin.com
收件人(To)	Abraham@yaoo.com

主题(Subject)	New Year Greetings
时间(Time)	Dec. 30th, 2021
附件(Attachment)	

Dear Mr. Abraham,

Please note that I will not be in office during Jan. 1st to 3rd, because of the New Year holiday.

For any questions, please call my mobile or send me short messages.

Happy New Year! Hope it brings you more success and happiness!

Best regards!

Aihua Zhang
Sales Manager
Guangzhou Hengxin Lighting Technology Co., Ltd.
24 Zhannan Road, Yuexiu District, Guangzhou, P. R. China 510010
Email：Zhangaihua@mail.hengxin.com
Tel：0086-020-86668420
Fax：0086-020-86668421
Mobile：13677885566
https://www.hengxin.com

1. 常用词汇

greeting	问候的话，祝词，贺词
note	留意，注意

2. 常用句型

(1) For any questions, please call my mobile or send me short messages.
(2) Happy New Year! Hope it brings you more success and happiness!

外贸业务指引

感恩节是美国和加拿大的全国性节日，美国将每年11月的第四个星期四定为感恩节，而加拿大将每年10月的第二个星期一定为感恩节。感恩节到圣诞节的这一个多月，是商家打折的促销旺季，这段时间内美国零售业的销售额能占据全年销售额的三分之一。所以感恩节前夕，可以给美国零售商一个问候，预祝他生意兴隆。除了美国、加拿大，世界上还有埃及、希腊等国家有自己独特的感恩节，但英国、法国等欧洲国家是没有感恩节的，所以千万不要向欧洲人祝贺，那是非常不礼貌的。

三、感恩节问候信函

发件人(From)	Zhangaihua@mail.hengxin.com
收件人(To)	Davis@yaoo.com
主题(Subject)	Thanksgiving Day Greetings
时间(Time)	Nov. 24th, 2021
附件(Attachment)	

Dear Mr. Davis,

Thanksgiving Day is coming. On behalf of all staff in our company, I wish you a huge retail in the holiday season of Thanksgiving Day & Christmas.

Good luck to you all!

Best regards!

Aihua Zhang
Sales Manager
Guangzhou Hengxin Lighting Technology Co., Ltd.
24 Zhannan Road, Yuexiu District, Guangzhou, P. R. China 510010
Email: Zhangaihua@mail.hengxin.com
Tel: 0086-020-86668420
Fax: 0086-020-86668421
Mobile: 13677885566
https://www.hengxin.com

1. 常用词汇

Thanksgiving Day	感恩节
on behalf of	代表
staff	全体员工,全体雇员
retail	零售

2. 常用句型

(1) On behalf of all staff in our company, I wish you a huge retail in the holiday season of Thanksgiving Day & Christmas.

(2) Good luck to you all!

外贸业务指引

每年的七八月份,从事外贸业务的人都会发现,他们与欧洲客户的沟通效率变得非常低,发邮件对方也不回。那是因为,欧洲客户已经开始休假了。欧洲很重视夏季假期,一般公司都有不成文的规定,在每年的7月末和8月初会给员工1~2周的带薪暑假,大部分公司的员工会轮流休假,有些公司甚至集体放假。工作上的事情,最好不要在休假期间打扰客户。我们可以提前询问客户什么时候结束休假,等假期结束后再与客户联系。

四、长假问候信函

发件人(From)	Zhangaihua@mail.hengxin.com
收件人(To)	Davis@yaoo.com
主题(Subject)	Holiday Greetings
时间(Time)	Aug. 2nd, 2021
附件(Attachment)	

Dear Mr. Davis,

I'm so glad to hear that you will be on holiday to Maldives next week.

When will you come back to office? I'd like to check with you the packing details of the items under order No. ABL-OP326.

Have a nice trip and enjoy your holiday!

Best regards!

Aihua Zhang
Sales Manager
Guangzhou Hengxin Lighting Technology Co., Ltd.
24 Zhannan Road, Yuexiu District, Guangzhou, P. R. China 510010
Email: Zhangaihua@mail.hengxin.com
Tel: 0086-020-86668420
Fax: 0086-020-86668421
Mobile: 13677885566
https://www.hengxin.com

1. 常用词汇

MALDIVES   马尔代夫

| packing details | 包装细节 |

2. 常用句型

(1)I'm so glad to hear that you will be on holiday to Maldives next week.

(2)Have a nice trip and enjoy your holiday!

外贸业务指引

在与客户交往的过程中,有时需要通过小礼物来表达自己的心意。一般情况下,礼物不需要太贵重,可以是一支玫瑰、一小盒咖啡、一碟自制的小饼干等。如果礼物价值过高,反而会让对方有压力,觉得欠了人情,或者没有办法接受。另外,带有中国传统文化气息的小礼品也比较受外国客户喜欢,如瓷器、泥人、木雕、刺绣、文房四宝等。

五、赠送礼物信函

发件人(From)	Zhangaihua@mail.hengxin.com
收件人(To)	Davis@yaoo.com
主题(Subject)	Meeting in HK
时间(Time)	Aug. 25th, 2021
附件(Attachment)	

Dear Mr. Davis,

Glad to hear that you're going to HK Disneyland with your daughter for her birthday next week. I prepared a tiny gift for her, a tin of cartoon biscuit.

Shall we have a dinner together if you have time then? What about the Thai food restaurant near the Victoria Peak?

Best regards!

Aihua Zhang
Sales Manager
Guangzhou Hengxin Lighting Technology Co., Ltd.
24 Zhannan Road, Yuexiu District, Guangzhou, P. R. China 510010
Email: Zhangaihua@mail.hengxin.com
Tel: 0086-020-86668420
Fax: 0086-020-86668421
Mobile: 13677885566
https://www.hengxin.com

1. 常用词汇

tiny	极小的,微小的
tin	有盖金属盒,金属食品盒
cartoon	动画片,卡通片
biscuit	饼干
Thai food	泰国菜
Victoria Peak	香港太平山

2. 常用句型

(1) I prepared a tiny gift for her, a tin of cartoon biscuit.

(2) Shall we have a dinner together if you have time then?

(3) What about the Thai food restaurant near the Victoria Peak?

外贸业务指引

升职加薪往往是职场中最值得高兴的事。一旦得知客户在公司的职位有升迁,应第一时间表示祝贺,感谢其在过去工作中的帮助和支持,并对未来的合作表示更有信心。很多跨国公司的管理非常严谨,一旦某人升职,都会由直属上司或人力资源部门撰写相关通知邮件,抄送全球所有供应商及合作伙伴。

六、升职祝贺信函

发件人(From)	Zhangaihua@mail.hengxin.com
收件人(To)	Davis@yaoo.com
主题(Subject)	Davis's promotion to SVP
时间(Time)	Sep. 6th, 2021
附件(Attachment)	

Dear Mr. Davis,

Congratulations on your promotion to Senior Vice President of Asia Pacific Hub.

We're sure that you deserve this honor due to your full experience in purchasing and HR administration. Thanks a lot for your support and trust in the past years! We'll always remember your kindness.

Back to business, could you please advise which guy will take over your work as buying head? Carolyn or Mason?

Best regards!

Aihua Zhang
Sales Manager
Guangzhou Hengxin Lighting Technology Co.，Ltd.
24 Zhannan Road，Yuexiu District，Guangzhou，P. R. China 510010
Email：Zhangaihua@mail.hengxin.com
Tel：0086-020-86668420
Fax：0086-020-86668421
Mobile：13677885566
https：//www.hengxin.com

1. 常用词汇

promotion	提拔，晋升
Senior Vice President	高级副总裁
Asia Pacific Hub	亚太中心
deserve	值得，应受
take over	接管，接手

2. 常用句型

（1）Congratulations on your promotion to Senior Vice President of Asia Pacific Hub.

（2）We're sure that you deserve this honor due to your full experience in purchasing and HR administration.

（3）Thanks a lot for your support and trust in the past years!

（4）Back to business，could you please advise which guy will take over your work as buying head?

外贸业务指引

得知客户生病，礼节上应该写一封私人邮件慰问一下，不论对方是否已经康复。邮件不需要太长，简单几句话点明主旨即可。邮件应以鼓励和关怀为目的，不是万不得已的情况下，这样的邮件里不应该出现跟工作有关的事宜。

七、生病慰问信函

发件人（From）	Zhangaihua@mail.hengxin.com
收件人（To）	Davis@yaoo.com
主题（Subject）	Take Care!
时间（Time）	Sep. 28th，2021

附件(Attachment)
Dear Mr. Davis, We learned from your assistant that you had been hospitalized. All of us here are hoping for your recovery ASAP. Don't worry about any pending cases. We will control everything well and discuss with your colleagues. Get well soon! May God bless you! Best regards! Aihua Zhang Sales Manager Guangzhou Hengxin Lighting Technology Co., Ltd. 24 Zhannan Road, Yuexiu District, Guangzhou, P. R. China 510010 Email:Zhangaihua@mail.hengxin.com Tel:0086-020-86668420 Fax:0086-020-86668421 Mobile:13677885566 https://www.hengxin.com

1. 常用词汇

take care	小心,保重
assistant	助理,助手
hospitalize	送入医院疗养(或治疗)
recovery	康复,痊愈
ASAP(as soon as possible)	尽快

2. 常用句型

(1) We learned from your assistant that you had been hospitalized.

(2) All of us here are hoping for your recovery ASAP.

(3) Don't worry about any pending cases.

(4) We will control everything well and discuss with your colleagues.

(5) Get well soon! May God bless you!

> **思政园地**
>
> (1)弘扬中华传统文化,提升爱国主义情怀,增强民族自豪感。
>
> 热爱中华民族的传统文化,在函电往来中向客户展示中华民族亲切、友好的形象。除了工作业务外,在节日问候、升职祝贺等日常沟通中注重增进与客户的感情,让客户感受到中华文明讲仁爱、重民本、守诚信的精神特质以及我国深厚的文化底蕴。
>
> (2)尊重文化的多元性,通过包容并进建立更高质量的合作伙伴关系。
>
> 坚持弘扬平等、互鉴、对话、包容的文明观,扫除傲慢与偏见,求同存异,优势互补,互利共赢。在弘扬中华传统文化的同时,吸收世界文化的多样性,处理好与外国客户的关系,共谋长远稳定发展。

课后习题

(一)单项选择

(1) Glad to hear that your company will be closed from Dec. 22nd, 2021 to Jan. 5th, 2022 (　　) Christmas holiday and New Year.

　　A. to　　　　　　B. for　　　　　　C. of　　　　　　D. on

(2) Please note that I will not be in office during Jan. 1st to 3rd, (　　) the New Year holiday.

　　A. as　　　　　　B. because of　　　C. because　　　　D. for

(3) (　　) any questions, please call my mobile or send me short messages.

　　A. For　　　　　　B. At　　　　　　C. On　　　　　　D. Of

(4) (　　) behalf of all staff in our company, I wish you a huge retail in the holiday season of Thanksgiving Day.

　　A. To　　　　　　B. At　　　　　　C. On　　　　　　D. In

(5) I'd like to check (　　) you the packing details of the items under order No. ABL-OP326.

　　A. to　　　　　　B. for　　　　　　C. with　　　　　　D. on

(6) What (　　) the Thai food restaurant near the Victoria Peak?

　　A. to　　　　　　B. of　　　　　　C. with　　　　　　D. about

(7) Congratulations (　　) your promotion to Senior Vice President of Asia Pacific Hub.

　　A. for　　　　　　B. at　　　　　　C. on　　　　　　D. of

(8) We're sure that you deserve this honor (　　) your full experience in purchasing and HR administration.

　　A. because　　　　B. due to　　　　C. as　　　　　　D. owing

(9) Don't worry (　　) any pending cases.

　　A. for　　　　　　B. about　　　　C. to　　　　　　D. of

(10) All of us here (　　) hoping for your recovery ASAP.

A. is B. was C. are D. were

(二)汉译英

(1)感谢你在过去一年的支持,祝你和你的家人圣诞快乐、新年快乐。

(2)由于新年假期,我将在1月1日至3日期间不在办公室。

(3)如果你到时有时间,我们一起吃个饭吧?

(4)祝贺您晋升为总经理。

(5)希望您能尽快康复。

(三)选择填空

(1)( ) and Happy New Year!

Many ( ) your supports in the past years, we wish our business will be ( ) in the coming years.

Last but not least, if you have any ( ) in the following days, please ( ) to contact me.

A. thanks for

B. further developed

C. feel free

D. Merry Christmas

E. questions

(2)We are thrilled and delighted to ( ) your marriage with Jack in Las Vegas next Saturday.

( ) here at No. 2 sales division want to send you our ( ) your wedding. Please also extend our regards to your husband.

Our sales rep Lynn is going to( ) your wedding party then and ( ) our tiny gifts to you.

A. transfer

B. All of us

C. know about

D. attend

E. congratulations on

(四)实训操作

4~5名同学为一组,其中1名同学扮演进口商,其他同学扮演出口商。

扮演出口商的同学结合任务一实训操作中的公司,通过互联网查找客户所在国家都有哪些比较重要的节日,并针对其中一个节日分别撰写给客户的祝福信函。

扮演进口商的同学选出写得最好的一封祝福信函并说明原因。

项目三　合同磋商与签订

Project Three: Contract Negotiation and Signing

学习目标

【思政目标】

培养学生具体问题具体分析以及透过现象看本质的能力；
培养学生诚实守信、实事求是的精神；
培养学生沟通协作、合作共赢等商务谈判业务素养；
培养学生正确的法律观念、良好的契约精神。

【知识目标】

掌握询盘、发盘、还盘、接受以及签订合同相关的常用英文词汇及句型；
掌握询盘、发盘、还盘、接受以及签订合同相关信函的结构与内容；
掌握报价的方法和技巧；
掌握还盘的方法和技巧。

【能力目标】

能够熟练阅读询盘函；
能够根据客户需求撰写详细专业的发盘函；
能够根据客户提出的交易条件撰写还盘函；
能够撰写接受以及签订合同相关的信函。

任务一 询盘

Task One：Enquiry

> **任务导入**
>
> 经过坚持不懈的努力,张爱华陆陆续续收到了不少客户的询盘。有的询盘专业详细,目的非常明确,对所需商品有具体的要求;而有的询盘却没有提供什么具体的信息,直接让她提供报价;甚至有的询盘什么都不问,仅仅是索要样品。张爱华仔细阅读了这些询盘,将它们分门别类,方便有针对性地回信。

外贸业务指引

询盘又叫询价,是指买方按需要向卖方进行的意向性订购询问活动(项目二中的开发信属于卖方询盘,本项目只详细讲解买方询盘,所以在此忽略卖方询盘的定义)。根据询盘涉及的内容可将其分为具体询盘和一般询盘两类:具体询盘往往都会列出产品的相关资料,如尺寸、型号、功能、相关参数、颜色、起订量、单价等明细,同时可能会附上图片或图纸;而一般询盘只是简单地阐述购买的意愿,没有具体的产品信息。

一、具体询盘(1)

发件人(From)	Albert@yaoo.com
收件人(To)	Zhangaihua@mail.hengxin.com
主题(Subject)	Enquiry for BP005,BP011,BP020
时间(Time)	Nov. 15th, 2021
附件(Attachment)	

Dear Ms. Zhang,

Thanks for your mail of Nov. 5th. After studying the night lights on your catalogue, we like the design and quality of your products, and are particularly interested in the item No. BP005, No. BP011 and No. BP020.

Please quote your best price, CIF Bangkok, for the above-mentioned three articles based on 1,000 pcs each, stating your shortest lead time.

Meanwhile, please send two samples of each item to our company before Nov. 30th. If your samples reach our quality level with reasonable price, we would like to place a large order with you.

We are looking forward to your early reply.

Best regards!

Martin Albert
Purchasing Manager

1. 常用词汇

quote	报价
Bangkok	曼谷
article	货物
state	陈述,说明,声明
lead time	订货至交货的时间,生产周期
place a large order	大量订购

2. 常用句型

(1) After studying the night lights on your catalogue, we like the design and quality of your products, and are particularly interested in the item No. BP005, No. BP011 and No. BP020.

(2) Please quote your best price, CIF Bangkok, for the above-mentioned three articles based on 1,000 pcs each, stating your shortest lead time.

(3) Meanwhile, please send two samples of each item to our company before Nov. 30th.

(4) If your samples reach our quality level with reasonable price, we would like to place a large order with you.

二、具体询盘(2)

发件人(From)	Smith@yaoo.com
收件人(To)	Zhangaihua@mail.hengxin.com
主题(Subject)	Glowing Bath Toy-TISI
时间(Time)	Nov. 20th, 2021
附件(Attachment)	

Dear Ms. Zhang,

I have read the specification sheet and catalogue you sent, and we are interested in your glowing bath toy No. BP005. As an initial order, we would like to purchase 1,000 pieces. Please quote your most competitive price.

Are you the manufacturer of this product? Do you have any certification for this product? For Thailand requirements, we will need TISI Certification for the item. Please send a sample of BP005 for us to test, and make sure it is suitable for Thailand standards.

Please send the sample with your business card to the following address:
Carry Smith
5/70, Mooban Nantatawee 4 Resort,
Moo 2, Mit Maitri 18/1,
Khu Fang Nuea, Nong Chok District,
Bangkok, 10530, Thailand.
Mobile: 0066 2 3180558
Using our FedEx account: 964864351.

Thanks and best regards!

Carry Smith
Purchasing Manager

1. 常用词汇

specification	规格,说明书
initial order	首次订单
purchase	买,购买,采购
Thailand	泰国(东南亚国家名)
TISI	泰国工业化标准协会
test	试验,测试
business card	名片
account	账户

2. 常用句型

(1) As an initial order, we would like to purchase 1,000 pieces.

(2) Are you the manufacturer of this product?

(3) Do you have any certification for this product? For Thailand requirements, we will need TISI Certification for the item.

(4) Please send a sample of BP005 for us to test, and make sure it is suitable for Thailand

standards.

(5)Please send the sample with your business card to the following address.

(6)Using our FedEx account：964864351.

营销知识链接

以上两封询盘函属于目标明确的专业型询盘。这类询盘通常有如下特点：(1)买家信息全面，包括来自的国家地区、公司名称、地址、电话、传真联系人；(2)需要的产品目标明确，有具体的品名、数量、交货条件、交货期等；(3)询问的问题专业，问题详细，但是内容简明扼要。这类询盘是值得我们高度注意的。这类买家比较专业，而且他们有采购此类产品的计划，所以针对这样的询盘要在第一时间专业、准确、全面、细致地回复。

拓展阅读

四大国际快递公司

四大国际快递公司包括：UPS(美国联合包裹运送服务公司，简称联合包裹)、DHL(德国敦豪国际公司，俗称中外运敦豪)、FedEx(美国联邦快递集团)、TNT(荷兰天地公司)。

1. UPS

优点：UPS是全球最大的国际快递公司，成立于美国。UPS时效快、服务好、服务地区广(可送达全球200多个国家和地区)、查询方便快捷、遇到问题能及时解决、可在线发货。在美国、加拿大、墨西哥的时效快，价格也较低。

缺点：UPS时效快、服务好，但运费也高，对托运物品限制严格。

时效：一般2~4个工作日可送达，而在美国一般48个小时就能送达。

2. DHL

优点：DHL是全球第二大国际快递巨头，成立于美国，总部设在德国，是全球快递、洲际运输和航空货运的领导者，也是全球海运和合同物流提供商。DHL到达区域多、查询方便、更新及时、解决问题速度快，运送21公斤以上物品有优势。在欧洲的时效快，在中东的时效也可以，价格一般。

缺点：运送小货运费贵不划算，对托运物品限制严格，拒收许多特殊商品。

时效：一般2~6个工作日可送达，欧洲一般3个工作日可送达，东南亚一般2个工作日可送达。

3. FedEx

优点：FedEx是全球第三大国际快递公司，提供隔夜快递、地面快递、重型货物运送、文件复印及物流服务，总部设于美国田纳西州。FedEx在东南亚很有实力，在中南美洲和欧洲的价格较有竞争力，但在其他地区较贵，其网站信息更新快、网络覆盖全面、查询方便快捷。

缺点：运费贵，对托运物品限制严格。

时效:一般 2~4 个工作日可送达。

4. TNT

优点:TNT 于 2016 年被 FedEx 收购,总部位于荷兰,在荷兰很有实力。TNT 时效快、清关能力强、查询方便、处理问题及时。它在西欧国家的清关能力是四大国际快递公司之首,比 DHL、UPS 都要强,在欧洲和亚洲可提供高效的递送网络。

缺点:价格比其他国际快递公司都要贵。如果货值高、货物贵重,要求时效快且通关能力强,可以选择 TNT。

三、一般询盘(1)

发件人(From)	Smith@yaoo.com
收件人(To)	Zhangaihua@mail.hengxin.com
主题(Subject)	Enquiry for Lights
时间(Time)	Nov. 20th, 2021
附件(Attachment)	

Dear Sirs,

We are one of the largest retailers in the US, and we are interested in adding some lights to our product range. We have learnt from www.alibaba.com that your company mainly specializes in light processing and selling. Your products such as bulb, indoor lighting and night light are exactly what we are looking for. Would you please send a catalogue with prices to Smith@yaoo.com?

Hope to hear your reply soon.

Best regards!

Carry Smith
Purchasing Manager

1. 常用词汇

retailer	零售商
product range	产品范围,产品种类
process	加工,处理
look for	寻找

2. 常用句型

(1)We are one of the largest retailers in the US, and we are interested in adding some lights to our product rang.

(2)Your products such as bulb, indoor lighting and night light are exactly what we are looking for.

(3)Would you please send a catalogue with prices to Smith@yaoo.com?

四、一般询盘(2)

发件人(From)	Smith@yaoo.com
收件人(To)	Zhangaihua@mail.hengxin.com
主题(Subject)	Enquiry for Lights
时间(Time)	Nov. 20th, 2021
附件(Attachment)	

Dear Sirs,

We got your name and email address from Alibaba and found that you can offer a wide range of lights.

Our company is one of the leading importers of lights in Canada. As there is a steady demand here for high quality lights, we would like you to send us as soon as possible your illustrated catalogues, samples, lowest price and all necessary information about the goods.

Should your quality be suitable and the price competitive, we will place a large order with you.

Best regards!

Carry Smith
Purchasing Manager

1. 常用词汇

a wide range of　　　　　　　多种多样的
leading　　　　　　　　　　主要的

2. 常用句型

(1)As there is a steady demand here for high quality lights, we would like you to send us as soon as possible your illustrated catalogues, samples, lowest price and all necessary information about the goods.

(2)Should your quality be suitable and the price competitive, we will place a large order with you.

营销知识链接

以上两封询盘函属于目标不明确的一般询盘。这类询盘往往没有说明具体的产品需求就直接让我们报价,或者向我们索要价目表或样品。这类询盘可能来自采购新手,他们本身对产品不是特别熟悉,所以难以对产品提出具体的要求;也可能来自目前尚未有明确采购目标的客户,他们想要通过询盘收集信息再做决定;甚至有可能来自别有用心、仅仅只是想要获得免费样品的客户。因此,我们要学会辨别客户,给予不同的回复。

思政园地

(1)具体问题具体分析,运用合适的方法解决问题。

要弄清楚询盘的目的以及向谁询盘,针对不同情况分别通过一般询盘或具体询盘进行咨询。比如,没有具体的产品需求,打算在旺季来临之前通过询盘调查来了解市场情况、供应商情况,可以通过一般询盘的方式进行咨询;又如,有目标性产品并且打算进一步了解相关具体交易条款,可以通过具体询盘的方式进行咨询。具体问题具体分析,能更高效地解决业务问题。

(2)透过现象看本质,分析询盘的性质。

收到询盘后,不要急于回复,要透过现象抓本质,分析清楚询盘的性质是一般询盘还是具体询盘。尤其对于具体询盘的邮件需要加以重视,该类型的询盘客户更有合作的可能性,要优先并详细地回复。

课后习题

(一)单项选择

(1)We would like to establish a long term business (　　) with you.
　　A. scope　　　　B. relations　　　　C. card　　　　D. school

(2)We are Australia's largest online tech-retailer, and we are interested in adding your auto rice cooker to our product (　　).
　　A. range　　　　B. extent　　　　C. area　　　　D. purview

(3)We have noticed your advertisement in www.qihuiwang.com and note with pleasure the (　　) of your company are exactly what we are looking for.
　　A. units　　　　B. pieces　　　　C. items　　　　D. columns

(4)We shall be glad if you will send us a copy of your illustrated (　　) and current price list.
　　A. procedure　　B. content　　　　C. description　　D. catalogue

(5)We are interested (　　) your products and shall be pleased to have a catalogue with a price list.
　　A. with　　　　B. in　　　　　　　C. to　　　　　　D. at

(6)Would you please send a (　　) of your product for us for quality test?
　　A. sample　　　B. photo　　　　　C. model　　　　D. duplicate

(7)Can you please (　　) your best price for your home use LaserJet M1136?
　　A. report　　　　B. declare　　　　C. quote　　　　D. announce

(8) Will you please give us detailed information of CIF prices, discounts and (　　) of payment?

  A. articles   B. conditions   C. terms   D. advices

(9) If your price is competitive, we will send you an (　　) for 5,000 sets.

  A. enquiry   B. offer   C. acceptance   D. order

(10) We look forward to your prompt (　　).

  A. reply   B. replying   C. replied   D. replies

(二)汉译英

(1) 我们是本市主要的电器进口商,现欲购买你方电扇。

(2) 我们对你方第 123 号瓷器感兴趣,请寄样品并告知所有必要的信息。

(3) 请报 CIF 纽约最低价,并说明最早的船期和付款方式。

(4) 请寄送产品的详细资料,包括尺寸、颜色和最低价格,并附寄送各种质料制成的样品。

(5) 本地区对高质量的手套有着稳定的需求。

(三)选择填空

(1) We are one of the (　　) of textile products and are well (　　) the local dealers in this line. (　　) your quality and prices are satisfactory, there are prospects of good sales in this area.

We would appreciate your sending us catalogues, price list or even (　　) if possible. When replying, please state your terms of payment and (　　) you would allow on purchases of quantities of more than 5,000 pieces of each item.

  A. Provided

  B. leading importers

  C. samples

  D. discount

  E. connected with

(2) At present, we are interested in Blanket Cover and shall be pleased if you will send us by airmail sample books and all necessary information on Blanket Cover, so as to (　　) materials and workmanship of your supplies.

Meanwhile, please (　　) us the lowest price (　　), inclusive of our 3% (　　), stating the earliest date of (　　).

  A. CIF London

  B. acquaint us with

  C. shipment

  D. quote

  E. commission

(四)实训操作

4~5 名同学为一组,其中 1 名同学扮演进口商,其他同学扮演出口商。

扮演进口商的同学结合项目二实训操作中的进出口商相关信息,撰写一封具体询盘函。

扮演出口商的同学分别点评这封询盘函的优缺点。

任务二 发盘

Task Two: Offer

任务导入

张爱华将询盘分好类之后，开始着手给客户回信。对于专业具体的询盘，张爱华相对应地也要回复一封专业详细的发盘函，这不仅要求她能够根据客户的要求准确地核算产品的价格，还要求她对产品的生产周期以及目前的航运状况了如指掌。而对于一般询盘，张爱华决定回信进一步询问客户的具体需求，同时在搜集客户信息的基础上，根据对客户需求的判断，主动向其推荐产品并报价。

外贸业务指引

外贸业务员在收到询盘后，应仔细研究并在第一时间给予回复，切不可拖沓，因为很多机会就是在等待中失去的。效率，往往会成为业务开发的关键。但有时要核算出准确的价格需要花费一些时间，比如向工厂确认产能与价格、联系货代咨询运费等，会导致很难立即向客户进行发盘。在这种情况下，我们应该第一时间回信，向客户说明实际情况，并告知什么时候会发盘给他。

一、回复具体询盘

发件人（From）	Zhangaihua@mail.hengxin.com
收件人（To）	Albert@yaoo.com
主题（Subject）	Re：Enquiry for BP005，BP011，BP020
时间（Time）	Nov. 15th, 2021
附件（Attachment）	

Dear Mr. Albert,

Thank you for your enquiry of Nov. 15th. I will check with our manager about the unit price for each item and give you reply with quotation sheet in 2 days. Any other questions, please also let me know.

Best regards!

```
Aihua Zhang
Sales Manager
Guangzhou Hengxin Lighting Technology Co., Ltd.
24 Zhannan Road, Yuexiu District, Guangzhou, P. R. China 510010
Email: Zhangaihua@mail.hengxin.com
Tel: 0086-020-86668420
Fax: 0086-020-86668421
Mobile: 13677885566
https://www.hengxin.com
```

1. 常用词汇

unit price　　　　　　　　　　单价

2. 常用句型

I will check with our manager about the unit price for each item and give you reply with quotation sheet in 2 days.

外贸业务指引

在我们核算出准确的价格之后,要及时撰写发盘函给客户。发盘是交易磋商的主要步骤,它是交易的一方向另一方提出出售或购买某种商品的各项交易条件,并愿意按这些条件达成交易、订立合同的一种书面或口头的肯定表示。做出发盘的人叫作"发盘人",接受发盘的人则叫作"受盘人"。

二、发盘(1)

发件人(From)	Zhangaihua@mail.hengxin.com
收件人(To)	Albert@yaoo.com
主题(Subject)	Offer for BP005, BP011, BP020
时间(Time)	Nov. 17th, 2021
附件(Attachment)	

Dear Mr. Albert,

Concerning your inquired item No. BP005, BP011 and BP020, we have sent the samples requested to you by FedEx with tracking number of 8640 0357 8857, you may trace it through www.fedex.com.

At your request, we offer as follows:

Item No. BP005：US＄ 3.5/pc，CIF Bangkok.
Item No. BP011：US＄ 6.5/pc，CIF Bangkok.
Item No. BP020：US＄ 17.5/pc，CIF Bangkok.

Kindly let us know your comment on samples. As we are receiving regular daily orders，it is quite probable that our ready stock may soon run out. It would be to your advantage to place orders without delay.

Thanks and best regards!

Aihua Zhang
Sales Manager
Guangzhou Hengxin Lighting Technology Co.，Ltd.
24 Zhannan Road，Yuexiu District，Guangzhou，P. R. China 510010
Email：Zhangaihua@mail.hengxin.com
Tel：0086-020-86668420
Fax：0086-020-86668421
Mobile：13677885566
https：//www.hengxin.com

1. 常用词汇

concerning	关于，涉及
tracking number	快递单号
trace	查出，找到，发现，追踪
ready stock	现货，库存
run out	用完，耗尽
to your advantage	对你有利

2. 常用句型

（1）Concerning your inquired item No. BP005，BP011 and BP020，we have sent the samples requested to you by FedEx with tracking number of 8640 0357 8857，you may trace it through www.fedex.com.

（2）At your request，we offer as follows：Item No. BP005：US＄ 3.5/pc，CIF Bangkok.

（3）As we are receiving regular daily orders，it is quite probable that our ready stock may soon run out.

（4）It would be to your advantage to place orders without delay.

• 请根据国际贸易专业知识，判断该发盘是否是一封有效的发盘函？

营销知识链接

报价，始终是外贸业务中最核心的问题，毕竟绝大多数情况下，价格是第一筛选条件。

价格计算很简单,一个公式套进去就能得出一个精确的数字。但是报价很复杂,因为价格报得是否合适,会直接决定你的客户是走还是留,以及是否有机会继续谈下去。价格报得过高,客户就会失去砍价的兴趣,直接淘汰我们;价格报低了,万一客户直接接受,自己可能吃亏,或者万一客户继续砍价,我们也没有继续降价的余地。这恐怕是绝大多数外贸业务员的共同心态。

所以,报价不能盲目,应该有一套明确的策略,对于卖方,报价前应提前确定好四个价格:成本价、最低价、目标成交价、报出价。

成本价即核算价格时该产品的成本。

最低价即成本价加上我们的最低利润。最低价是客户讨价还价时我们能够给予的底限,这是谈判的最后砝码,只要这个底限存在,我们就永远不会迷茫。如果客户砍价,我们就能很清楚地知道我们是否还能退让;如果被逼到了这个底限,我们就可以很坚决地告诉客户,无法再降!所以,报价时就应该确定好最低价。

目标成交价即我们希望和客户成交的价格。这个价格往往高于最低价,但有时也可能等于最低价,要根据客户的情况来调整。

报出价即我们在发盘中报给客户的价格。报出价往往比目标成交价要高一些,以此留下和客户讨价还价的空间。但现实当中,并不是所有的客户都喜欢讨价还价,有可能因为我们报出的价格虚高,客户就直接不理我们了。所以,仍然需要根据对行业和客户的分析,进行最终的报价。

三、发盘(2)

发件人(From)	Zhangaihua@mail.hengxin.com
收件人(To)	Albert@yaoo.com
主题(Subject)	Offer for BP005, BP011, BP020
时间(Time)	Nov. 17th, 2021
附件(Attachment)	

Dear Mr. Albert,

With reference to your enquiry of Nov. 15th, we take pleasure in making the following offer. Please note that this offer is subject to our final confirmation.

1. Article: BP005 Glowing Bath Toy.
   Pattern: whale.
   Price: US$ 3.5 /pc, CIF Bangkok.
   Quantity: 1,000 pcs.
   Packing: 1 piece in a box, 65 boxes in a carton.

2. Article: BP011 Rainbow Unicorn Night Light.
   Pattern: unicorn.
   Price: US$ 6.5 /pc, CIF Bangkok.

> Quantity: 1,000 pcs.
>
> Packing: 1 piece in a box, 20 boxes in a carton.
>
> 3. Article: BP020 Sleepy Chick.
>   Pattern: chick.
>   Price: US$ 17.5 /pc, CIF Bangkok.
>   Quantity: 1,000 pcs.
>   Packing: 1 piece in a box, 20 boxes in a carton.
>
> Date of Shipment: in December, 2021.
> Terms of Payment: 30% deposit and the balance paid against the copy of shipping documents.
>
> Besides, we have sent the samples requested to you by FedEx with tracking number of 8640 0357 8857, you may trace it through www.fedex.com.
>
> We look forward to receiving your order.
>
> Best regards!
>
> Aihua Zhang
> Sales Manager
> Guangzhou Hengxin Lighting Technology Co., Ltd.
> 24 Zhannan Road, Yuexiu District, Guangzhou, P. R. China 510010
> Email: Zhangaihua@mail.hengxin.com
> Tel: 0086-020-86668420
> Fax: 0086-020-86668421
> Mobile: 13677885566
> https://www.hengxin.com

1. 常用词汇

with reference to	关于
subject to	以……为条件,以……为有效
confirmation	证实,确认
carton	纸板箱
unicorn	(传说中的)独角兽
chick	雏鸟,(尤指)雏鸡,小鸡
deposit	订金
balance	余额,尾款

2. 常用句型

(1) Please note that this offer is subject to our final confirmation.

(2)Packing：1 piece in a box，65 boxes in a carton.

(3)Terms of Payment：30% deposit and the balance paid against the copy of shipping documents.

• 请根据国际贸易专业知识,判断该发盘是实盘还是虚盘?

营销知识链接

根据《联合国国际货物销售合同公约》的规定,一项有效的发盘的内容至少应包括产品名称、价格和数量,但在外贸实践中,产品的包装、发货期、支付方式等交易条件都会对产品的价格产生一定影响,所以,在发盘时应尽可能把这些信息都提供完整。一封完整详细的发盘函,一方面可以体现出我们的专业性,另外一方面可以推进交易磋商的进度,避免就一个问题反复纠缠。因此,一封完整专业的发盘函,应包括产品名称、价格、数量、包装、发货期、支付方式等,必要时还可以包括发盘有效期、产品详细参数及优势等。

四、发盘(3)

发件人(From)	Zhangaihua@mail.hengxin.com
收件人(To)	Albert@yaoo.com
主题(Subject)	Offer for BP005，BP011，BP020
时间(Time)	Nov. 17th，2021
附件(Attachment)	Hengxin Quotation Sheet QT20210155 for Night Lights

Dear Mr. Albert，

Thank you for your enquiry of Nov. 15th. At your request，we are making you the enclosed offer，which is valid for 3 months.

The total amount is US＄27,500，if you purchase 1,000 pieces of each item. Meanwhile，you can earn a 2% discount on orders exceeding US＄35,000 in value. We desire to call your attention to our special offer. You will find it both good in quality and reasonable in price.

Meanwhile，four samples have been sent to you today by FedEx with tracking No. 8640 0357 8857，hoping they can turn out to your satisfaction.

Any orders you place with us will be processed promptly.

Best regards！

Aihua Zhang
Sales Manager
Guangzhou Hengxin Lighting Technology Co., Ltd.
24 Zhannan Road, Yuexiu District, Guangzhou, P. R. China 510010
Email: Zhangaihua@mail.hengxin.com
Tel: 0086-020-86668420
Fax: 0086-020-86668421
Mobile: 13677885566
https://www.hengxin.com

Guangzhou Hengxin Lighting Technology Co., Ltd.
Main Products: Bulb, Indoor Lighting, Night Light, Feather Light, Table Lamp, Decorative Light, Smart Home

Date: Nov. 17th, 2021
To: Martin Albert/Thomas
From: Aihua Zhang/Guangzhou Hengxin
QT No. QT20210155

BP005 Glowing Bath Toy	whale	1,000	US$ 3.5/pc, CIF Bangkok	1 piece in a box, 65 boxes in a carton	USD 3,500.00
BP011 Rainbow Unicorn Night Light	unicorn	1,000	US$ 6.5/pc, CIF Bangkok	1 piece in a box, 20 boxes in a carton	USD 6,500.00
BP020 Sleepy Chick	chick	1,000	US$ 17.5/pc, CIF Bangkok	1 piece in a box, 20 boxes in a carton	USD 17,500.00
Total Amount					USD 27,500.00

Date of Shipment: in December, 2021.
Terms of Payment: 30% deposit and the balance paid against the copy of shipping documents.

Aihua Zhang
Sales Manager

```
Guangzhou Hengxin Lighting Technology Co., Ltd.
24 Zhannan Road, Yuexiu District, Guangzhou, P. R. China 510010
Email: Zhangaihua@mail.hengxin.com
Tel: 0086-020-86668420
Fax: 0086-020-86668421
Mobile: 13677885566
https://www.hengxin.com
```

1. 常用词汇

valid	有效的
amount	金额
exceed	超过，超出
turn out	被发现是
process	处理
promptly	迅速地，及时地

2. 常用句型

(1) At your request, we are making you the enclosed offer, which is valid for 3 months.

(2) The total amount is US $ 27,500, if you purchase 1,000 pieces of each item.

(3) Meanwhile, you can earn a 2% discount on orders exceeding US $ 35,000 in value.

(4) Meanwhile, four samples have been sent to you today by FedEx with tracking No. 8640 0357 8857, hoping they can turn out to your satisfaction.

(5) Any orders you place with us will be processed promptly.

营销知识链接

当需要报价的产品种类比较多时，直接在邮件正文里一一报价，会导致邮件太长，不方便客户保存、分析相关资料，因此以附件的形式发送报价单给客户将是一个不错的选择。报价单除了报价之外，还可以起到方便客户统计资料、进行备忘的作用。因此，在制作报价单时，应注意以下格式和细节。

(1) 可以把一些较为关键的内容写进邮件正文里，如总报价、突出的优势等，从而吸引客户打开报价单。

(2) 为了避免因客户使用的电脑系统或办公软件不同导致文件出现乱码或格式错乱，可同时发送 word 或 excel 版报价单和 PDF 或图片版报价单给客户。

(3) 报价单的命名应包含公司名称和产品名称，例如 Hengxin Quotation Sheet for Night Lights，保证客户无论什么时候看到我们的报价单，都能够知道这份报价单是关于什么产品的，以及来自于哪个公司。

(4) 可以给报价单设置页眉、页脚，加入自己公司的标志、名称、电话、传真、邮箱、理念、口号等，这是用来提升企业形象的一种方法。

(5) 在报价单上标明制作时间、抬头、有效期，以及公司名称、地址、本人联系方式等各种基本信息。

（6）以表格的形式进行报价，清晰明了，并且应包含商品名称、价格、数量、包装、交货期、支付方式等重要交易条件。

（7）适当加入必要的图片，如产品图片、装箱图片、工厂图片、认证证书等等，做到图文并茂。

外贸业务指引

对于一般询盘，因为客户所需要的产品不明确，所以我们很难直接进行准确的报价。我们可以写信进一步询问客户的具体要求，也可以搜集整理客户信息，分析客户需求，推荐产品给客户并报价。

五、询问客户具体需求

发件人（From）	Zhangaihua@mail.hengxin.com
收件人（To）	Smith@yaoo.com
主题（Subject）	Re：Enquiry for Lights/Hengxin
时间（Time）	Nov. 21st, 2021
附件（Attachment）	

Dear Mr. Smith,

Thank you for your enquiry of Nov. 20th. Please find our product catalogue in attachment. All our indoor lighting, night light and feather light are popular. I will make an exact offer to you if you could give me the following information:

1. Item No..
2. Quantity.
3. Desired time of delivery.
4. Requirements of packing.

By the way, we work on OEM orders. If any special requirements, please let me know and I will give you offer as per your request.

Thanks and best regards!

Aihua Zhang
Sales Manager
Guangzhou Hengxin Lighting Technology Co., Ltd.

24 Zhannan Road，Yuexiu District，Guangzhou，P. R. China 510010
Email：Zhangaihua@mail.hengxin.com
Tel：0086-020-86668420
Fax：0086-020-86668421
Mobile：13677885566
https：//www.hengxin.com

1.常用词汇

exact　　　　　　　　　　　精确的
as per　　　　　　　　　　　按照，依据

2.常用句型

（1）Please find our product catalogue in attachment.

（2）I will make an exact offer to you if you could give me the following information.

（3）If any special requirements，please let me know and I will give you offer as per your request.

营销知识链接

向客户推荐产品并报价，相当于把开发信和发盘的内容整合进同一封信里，既要向客户说明推荐该产品的理由，即写清楚产品的优势，还要进行完整专业的报价。推荐产品的前提是了解客户的需求，因此，首先需要对客户进行充分的调研和分析，可以直接写信询问客户的联系方式、公司网站、购买用途等等。如果客户一一回复了我们的问题，说明该客户是有诚意购买我们的产品的，我们就要好好研究其提供的信息，做出有针对性的发盘。如果客户不回信，我们可以将我们公司的热销产品推荐给他。

外贸业务指引

还有一些询盘，客户没有提供与交易相关的任何信息，直接就向我们索要样品。如果有顾虑，担心白白浪费掉一个样品，我们可以让客户承担快递费，这样对双方都公平。并且我们还可以以此判断客户是否有购买产品的可能性，如果他不再回信给我们，那基本上可以确定这个客户并不是真心想要购买产品，我们也就不必邮寄样品给他了；如果客户愿意承担快递费，那我们就可以提供样品并做好进一步营销的准备。

六、请客户支付快递费

发件人（From）	Zhangaihua@mail.hengxin.com
收件人（To）	Smith@yaoo.com
主题（Subject）	Re：Enquiry for Lights/Hengxin

时间（Time）	Nov. 21st，2021
附件（Attachment）	

Dear Mr. Smith，

Thank you for your enquiry of Nov. 20th and interest in our products. We can provide you FREE samples as the best support for our business. But the postage will be for your account. So，could you please inform us your account number of UPS or FedEx or other express?

Thank you for your cooperation. Looking forward to hearing from you soon.

Best regards！

Aihua Zhang
Sales Manager
Guangzhou Hengxin Lighting Technology Co.，Ltd.
24 Zhannan Road，Yuexiu District，Guangzhou，P. R. China 510010
Email：Zhangaihua@mail.hengxin.com
Tel：0086-020-86668420
Fax：0086-020-86668421
Mobile：13677885566
https://www.hengxin.com

1. 常用词汇

postage	邮资，邮费
for your account	由你方支付
express	快件服务，快递服务，快运服务

2. 常用句型

（1）We can provide you FREE samples as the best support for our business.

（2）But the postage will be for your account.

（3）Could you please inform us your account number of UPS or FedEx or other express?

拓展阅读

国际快递到付账号

如果我们提供免费样品，而让客户承担快递费的话，应向客户索要其国际快递到付账号，这样快递公司就可以从其账号里直接扣除快递费。

1. UPS 国际快递公司到付账号

全球 UPS 账号为 6 位数。客户一般是每月或者每半年和 UPS 结算一次，UPS 会给客户一张账单,只有客户在账单上签字,UPS才能从他的银行卡或者信用卡里扣钱。但是在美国,任何人都可以随便在网上申请UPS账号,UPS的客服中心也很难核实账号的真假,就算账号是真的,只要客户不签字拒付,UPS就会找发货人来收快递费。

2. FedEx国际快递公司到付账号

要使用FedEx的到付账号,我们需要先以公司的名义注册账号,然后支付保证金给快递公司。如果客户收到样品并支付了快递费,保证金会在6个月后退回。如果客户拒付,那么将直接从保证金中扣除快递费。

3. TNT国际快递公司到付账号

使用TNT快递到付,需要我们把寄件人的地址和电话告知国外客户,请国外客户向当地的TNT公司发出取件通知,国外的TNT再通知中国的TNT公司,最后通知到寄件人,这时就可以寄件了。这种操作模式需要的时间可能会比较长,但是比较保险,可以省下保证金。

4. DHL国际快递公司到付账号

DHL的到付做得最好,它的账号分为两种:一种是全球账号,一种是当地账号。全球账号以96或者95开头,其有效性可以预先查询,账号本身就有预存款,运费直接从该账号中扣除,只要客户提供的是全球账号就基本没有问题,拒付率极低。对于当地账号,首先需要寄件人与收件人达成协议,然后由寄件人通知收件人包裹的大概重量和体积,并请收件人向当地的DHL发出取件通知,再由收件人所在地的DHL通知寄件人所在地的DHL,最后由寄件人所在地的DHL通知寄件人,并将包裹寄出。

外贸业务指引

一般情况下,我们不会向客户收取样品费。但如果客户在没有下订单的情况下,要求我们为其专门定做样品,且样品有专门的包装,需要投入各种制版费、操作费等,金额还不小,我们就可以对客户实话实说,并酌情收取样品费。

七、请客户支付样品费

发件人(From)	Zhangaihua@mail.hengxin.com
收件人(To)	Smith@yaoo.com
主题(Subject)	Re: Enquiry for Lights/Hengxin
时间(Time)	Nov. 21st, 2021
附件(Attachment)	

Dear Mr. Smith,

Thank you for your enquiry of Nov. 20th. Because we should make the new samples strictly according to your logo printing, please pay for the film charge USD 300 by your side. After order placed, you could deduct this cost when paying the balance. Enclosed please find our bank account file. Please advise your opinion.

Thanks and best regards!

Aihua Zhang
Sales Manager
Guangzhou Hengxin Lighting Technology Co., Ltd.
24 Zhannan Road, Yuexiu District, Guangzhou, P. R. China 510010
Email：Zhangaihua@mail.hengxin.com
Tel：0086-020-86668420
Fax：0086-020-86668421
Mobile：13677885566
https://www.hengxin.com

1. 常用词汇

film charge	菲林费，制版费
deduct	扣除
bank account	银行账户

2. 常用句型

(1) Because we should make the new samples strictly according to your logo printing, please pay for the film charge USD 300 by your side.

(2) After order placed, you could deduct this cost when paying the balance.

思政园地

(1) 培养诚实守信、实事求是的精神。

首先，注意发盘的完整性，内容应包括币种、价格、单位、贸易术语四要素，力求做到意思准确清晰。其次，注意报价水平合适，过低的价格容易导致亏损，过高的价格容易错失商机，应从企业实际出发合理计算有竞争力的价格。再次，在撰写回复询盘同时向对方发盘的函电时，需要回复客户咨询的问题，注意不要遗漏，让客户感受到我方对该业务的重视以及我方办事的专业水平。

(2) 培养良好的时间观念以及灵敏的市场洞察力。

注意发盘的性质，若为实盘要写清楚发盘的有效期，若为虚盘则注意写上以我方确认为准或以库存为准等表达。如果市场较为稳定，希望客户接受后就可以直接展开业务流程，可以向客户发实盘，注意形成良好的时间观念，促使客户及时下单或反馈问题，以提高工作效率；如果市场波动较大，希望保留发盘的主动权以备及时调整报价，则可以向客户发虚盘。

课后习题

(一)单项选择

(1)(　　) your Enquiry No. HS073，we are sending you a catalogue and a sample book for your reference.
  A. According B. As per C. As D. About

(2)We are sending you the samples (　　) requested.
  A. be B. are C. as D. for

(3)We would make you the following offer, subject to your reply (　　) us not later than November 25.
  A. reach B. reaching C. reaches D. being reached

(4)We cannot make you an offer, as the goods are (　　).
  A. without any stock B. no stock
  C. less in stock D. out of stock

(5)In view of the large demand of the goods, we suggest you to (　　) fast and place an order with us as soon as possible.
  A. decide B. take action C. work D. run

(6)This offer is a (　　), which has some exchanges of terms and conditions in a certain time limit.
  A. firm offer B. non-firm offer C. bid D. counter-offer

(7)This price is (　　) of your 5% commission.
  A. includes B. covering C. inclusive D. including

(8)Provided we receive your order before October 30, we will make you a firm offer (　　) delivery in November (　　) the price quoted.
  A. for, on B. for, at C. of, according D. of, at

(9)We are now (　　) a position to supply any quantity of the captioned goods from stock (　　) the exact specification of your sample.
  A. in, to B. at, with C. at, for D. in, of

(10)Rubber Gloves are packed (　　) cartons (　　)100 pairs each.
  A. in, of B. of, for C. with, of D. to, for

(二)汉译英

(1)贵公司昨天的询盘收悉，现就我方洗衣机报盘如下。

(2)作为回复，我方报盘如下，以我方最终确认为准。

(3)详见附件的报价单，随附一份产品宣传单，以便您了解产品的详细信息。

(4)我方已经通过联邦快递向您发送了您所需的样品,快递号码为8640 0357 8857,您可以通过www.fedex.com查询。

(5)我司可以提供免费样品,但是邮费需要你方来支付。

(三)选择填空

(1)Thank you for your (　　) of April 3 about our T-shirts for men and women.

We have pleasure in (　　) our latest catalogue and (　　). We hope you will find it of much interest.

If you require any further (　　), please do not hesitate to (　　) us.

A. price list

B. enclosing

C. contact

D. enquiry

E. detail

(2)We thank you for your fax of Nov. 16 (　　) our 100% Cotton Men's Jackets.

We are making you (　　) for 5,000 pieces of the item (　　) per piece FOB Shanghai for shipment in Jan. 2014. Payment by irrevocable L/C at sight is required. This offer (　　) your reply reaching us on or before Nov. 25, our time.

Please note that we have (　　) our best price and are unable to entertain any counter-offer.

If you need any further information, please contact us.

A. an offer

B. is subject to

C. inquiring for

D. quoted

E. at US＄30.00

(四)实训操作

4～5名同学为一组,其中1名同学扮演进口商,其他同学扮演出口商。

扮演出口商的同学针对任务一实训操作中的进口商询盘,分别撰写发盘函。

扮演进口商的同学选出写得最好的一封发盘函并说明原因

任务三　还盘

Task Three：Counter-offer

任务导入

2021年11月21日,张爱华收到了客户Martin Albert的回信,他认为张爱华给出的价格太高,并指出越南的供应商可以提供更低的价格给他们,所以希望张爱华降价8%成交。而对张爱华来说,降价5%之后的价格是其能够接受的最低成交价。张爱华应该怎样回信给客户呢?而客户又会做出怎样的反应呢?最终他们是否能够成交呢?

外贸业务指引

还盘是受盘人不同意或不完全同意发盘中的内容或条件而提出自己的修改意见或条件的表示,还盘其实是对发盘的部分或完全拒绝。还盘可以明确使用"还盘"字样,也可以不使用,只在内容中表示对发盘的修改。还盘可以针对价格,也可以针对交易商品的品质、数量、装运、支付等。还盘时,一般只针对原发盘提出不同意见和需要修改的部分,已同意的内容在还盘中可以省略。在外贸实务中,还盘阶段是交易磋商中持续时间最长的阶段,一笔业务通常需要经过多次还盘才能达成最后协议,但也可能谈不拢。

一、进口商还盘(1)

发件人(From)	Albert@yaoo.com
收件人(To)	Zhangaihua@mail.hengxin.com
主题(Subject)	Re:Offer for BP005,BP011,BP020
时间(Time)	Nov. 21st, 2021
附件(Attachment)	

Dear Ms. Zhang,

Thanks for your offer of Nov. 18th and samples which are excellent both in design and quality.

However, we regret to inform you that your price is rather on the high side and out of line with the prevailing market level here. And you may be aware that some Vietnamese suppliers could offer lower prices.

To step up the trade, we will place regular orders if you could reduce your price by 8%, that is:
BP005:US$ 3.22/pc, CIF Bangkok.
BP011:US$ 5.98/pc, CIF Bangkok.
BP020:US$ 16.1/pc, CIF Bangkok.

You will find it worthwhile to make a concession. We await your favorable reply with keen interest.

Best regards!

Martin Albert
Purchasing Manager

1. 常用词汇

on the high side	偏高
out of line with	跟……不一致

prevailing	普遍的，盛行的，流行的
aware	知道的，意识到的
Vietnamese	越南的，越南人的
step up	加强，促成
regular order	长期订单
reduce	减少，降低
worthwhile	值得的
concession	让步，妥协，降价

2. 常用句型

(1) However, we regret to inform you that your price is rather on the high side and out of line with the prevailing market level here.

(2) And you may be aware that some Vietnamese suppliers could offer lower prices.

(3) To step up the trade, we will place regular orders if you could reduce your price by 8%.

(4) You will find it worthwhile to make a concession.

外贸业务指引

客户讨价还价是每个业务员都难免会碰到的情况，有的客户根据产品和数量的不同砍价，有的客户根据市场定位砍价，有的客户根据以往的采购经验砍价，甚至还有客户先乱砍一通，然后再通过货比三家来压出最低价。这都需要业务员根据经验来判断客户的砍价究竟是真实且有依据的，还是带有水分的。回复的时候也要有针对性，不论降价还是维持原价，甚至是涨价，都需要有合理的理由，要有理有据。

二、出口商还盘(1)

发件人(From)	Zhangaihua@mail.hengxin.com
收件人(To)	Albert@yaoo.com
主题(Subject)	Re：Re：Offer for BP005，BP011，BP020
时间(Time)	Nov. 22nd, 2021
附件(Attachment)	

Dear Mr. Albert,

Thank you for your email of Nov. 21st which requested an 8% discount, but I regret to inform you that we can't make such a great discount. The material of our night lights is food-grade silicone, which can be used as infant teethers and is no harm to the baby's health. So, it is more expensive than the ordinary-silicone night lights of the Vietnamese suppliers.

In addition, I believe that you know the cost of labor, raw material and shipment are all increasing affected by COVID-19 epidemic, so that our product cost increased accordingly.

However, in order to initiate our long and mutual benefit business relations, we decide to make an exception to give you 3% discount if you can increase the order quantity to 1,300 pcs each item, which is the best we can offer.

1. Article: BP005 Glowing Bath Toy.
   Pattern: whale.
   Price: US$ 3.4/pc, CIF Bangkok.
   Quantity: 1,300 pcs.
   Packing: 1 piece in a box, 65 boxes in a carton.

2. Article: BP011 Rainbow Unicorn Night Light.
   Pattern: unicorn.
   Price: US$ 6.3/pc, CIF Bangkok.
   Quantity: 1,300 pcs.
   Packing: 1 piece in a box, 20 boxes in a carton.

3. Article: BP020 Sleepy Chick.
   Pattern: chick.
   Price: US$ 16.9/pc, CIF Bangkok.
   Quantity: 1,300 pcs.
   Packing: 1 piece in a box, 20 boxes in a carton.

In view of the above, we suggest that you accept our offer without delay as the price might soon soar up. Looking forward to your early acceptance.

Best regards!

Aihua Zhang
Sales Manager
Guangzhou Hengxin Lighting Technology Co., Ltd.
24 Zhannan Road, Yuexiu District, Guangzhou, P. R. China 510010
Email: Zhangaihua@mail.hengxin.com
Tel: 0086-020-86668420
Fax: 0086-020-86668421
Mobile: 13677885566
https://www.hengxin.com

1. 常用词汇

silicone	硅胶,硅酮

raw material	原材料
COVID-19 epidemic	新冠肺炎疫情
accordingly	相应地
initiate	开始,发起,创始
mutual benefit	互惠互利
make an exception	破例
soar	急升,猛涨

2. 常用句型

(1) Thank you for your email of Nov. 21st which requested an 8% discount, but I regret to inform you that we can't make such a great discount.

(2) I believe that you know the cost of labor, raw material and shipment are all increasing affected by COVID-19 epidemic, so that our product cost increased accordingly.

(3) In order to initiate our long and mutual benefit business relations, we decide to make an exception to give you 3% discount if you can increase the order quantity to 1,300 pcs each item.

(4) In view of the above, we suggest that you accept our offer without delay as the price might soon soar up.

营销知识链接

初次报价以后,来来回回地讨价还价是很常见的。卖方希望获得更高的利润,买方希望买到更便宜的产品,这就需要多轮的价格拉锯,最后大家在谈判和磨合中找到双方都能接受的某个折中点。为了更好地应对客户的讨价还价,我们首先要搞清楚客户不接受我们价格的原因:(1)如果是有同行报了比我们更低的价格,那么我们可以直接把价格降到客户要求的水平,但同时提出交换条件,比如提高采购量、增加预付款等,也可以在仔细研究竞争对手的产品后,稍微降价,同时详细阐述我们的产品相较于竞争对手的差异与优势;(2)如果是客户的预算不够,那么我们可以询问客户是否能够增加预算,或者推荐给他另外一款功能相同但配置较低的产品;(3)如果是客户觉得我们的产品不值这个价,那么我们可以将产品的各项成本构成拆分,通过具体的数据向客户证明产品的价值所在,同时再次向客户强调我们的优势。

外贸业务指引

除了就价格问题进行还盘之外,进口商还往往会在采购数量、交货期、支付方式等方面进行讨价还价。这就需要我们在还盘阶段对这些主要的交易条件进行综合考虑。

三、进口商还盘(2)

发件人(From)	Albert@yaoo.com
收件人(To)	Zhangaihua@mail.hengxin.com

主题(Subject)	Re：Re：Re：Offer for BP005，BP011，BP020
时间(Time)	Nov. 24th, 2021
附件(Attachment)	

Dear Ms. Zhang,

Thanks a lot for your detailed explanation and the efforts to support us. We agree to increase the quantity of each item to 1,300 pcs.

But we hope you could reduce the price by 5% and revise your payment terms. It's our company's policy that we never accept deposit payment, as this might bring us some risks and tie up our funds. Therefore, we suggest you accept payment by 100% T/T against the copy of shipping documents.

Your priority to consideration of the above request and giving us an early favorable reply will be highly appreciated.

Best regards!

Martin Albert
Purchasing Manager

1. 常用词汇

detailed explanation	详细解释
revise	改变，修改
tie up	占用
fund	资金，钱款
priority	优先
favorable	赞成的，赞许的

2. 常用句型

(1) Thanks a lot for your detailed explanation and the efforts to support us.

(2) But we hope you could reduce the price by 5% and revise your payment terms.

(3) Therefore, we suggest you accept payment by 100% T/T against the copy of shipping documents.

(4) Your priority to consideration of the above request and giving us an early favorable reply will be highly appreciated.

外贸业务指引

为了更好地应对客户的还盘，我们在报价阶段就应该将每项交易条件写完整，即将价格与采购数量、交货期、支付方式、包装等的对应关系写清楚,避免被客户牵着鼻子走。除了价格之外,支付方式的谈判对业务员的外贸专业知识的要求也是比较高的。我们需要对各种支付方式的风险和操作方式了如指掌,才能够分辨出何种支付方式对我方有利,何种支付方式风险巨大,才能够有理有据地说服客户接受我方的支付方式。

四、出口商还盘(2)

发件人(From)	Zhangaihua@mail.hengxin.com
收件人(To)	Albert@yaoo.com
主题(Subject)	Re：Re：Re：Re：Offer for BP005, BP011, BP020
时间(Time)	Nov. 25th, 2021
附件(Attachment)	

Dear Mr. Albert,

Thank you for your email of Nov. 24th requesting a change in the terms of payment. But we regret we can't accept your proposal which will bring us risks too, especially for initial orders.

As you know, our price is very low. Nobody will do the business without enough profit. However, to show our sincerity to cooperate with you, if you can accept 100% irrevocable documentary L/C at sight in seller's favor, we will make a concession again and reduce the price by 5%.

The best we can offer is as follows.
1. Terms of Payment: 30% deposit and the balance paid against the copy of shipping documents.
   BP005: US$ 3.4 /pc, CIF Bangkok.
   BP011: US$ 6.3 /pc, CIF Bangkok.
   BP020: US$ 16.9 /pc, CIF Bangkok.

2. Terms of Payment: 100% irrevocable documentary L/C at sight in seller's favor. The shipment can only be made within 1 month after receipt of your L/C.
   BP005: US$ 3.3 /pc, CIF Bangkok.
   BP011: US$ 6.2 /pc, CIF Bangkok.
   BP020: US$ 16.6 /pc, CIF Bangkok.

Please consider and inform us which way is better for you. Looking forward to your early acceptance.

Best regards!

```
Aihua Zhang
Sales Manager
Guangzhou Hengxin Lighting Technology Co., Ltd.
24 Zhannan Road, Yuexiu District, Guangzhou, P. R. China 510010
Email：Zhangaihua@mail.hengxin.com
Tel：0086-020-86668420
Fax：0086-020-86668421
Mobile：13677885566
https://www.hengxin.com
```

1. 常用词汇

proposal	提议，建议
sincerity	真诚，真挚
irrevocable	不可撤销的
at sight	即期
in seller's favor	以卖方为受益人

2. 常用句型

(1) But we regret we can't accept your proposal which will bring us risks too, especially for initial orders.

(2) However, to show our sincerity to cooperate with you, if you can accept 100% irrevocable documentary L/C at sight in seller's favor, we will make a concession again and reduce the price by 5%.

(3) The shipment can only be made within one month after receipt of your L/C.

(4) Please consider and inform us which way is better for you.

营销知识链接

如果公司的支付方式比较灵活，那么我们就可以根据客户的具体情况，去谈一个双方都能接受的支付方式。想要让客户接受我方的支付方式，往往需要一个合理的理由来说服客户，除特殊情况外，一般情况下尽量不要以行业规矩或公司规定作为理由，因为这种理由好像在指责客户不懂行业规矩一样，并且每个公司都有自己的规定，如果买卖双方都坚持自己的公司规定，只会导致谈判进入僵局。

我们可以把付款方式和价格或交货期放在一起谈，对我方来说风险大的付款方式对应较高的价格或较晚的交货期，反之应对应低价或较近的交货期，让客户选择；也可以将客户提出的支付方式和我方的支付方式进行对比分析，从而找出一种折中的支付方式，从公平互惠的角度来说服客户；甚至可以放低姿态，以公司发展或原材料涨价导致资金紧张为理由，恳请客户给予支持。谈支付方式和谈价格一样，方法各种各样，不一而足，需要我们在实践中不断尝试并总结。

思政园地

（1）培养沟通协作、合作共赢等商务谈判业务素养。

在还盘阶段，要注意与客户进行有效沟通，一方面要表达清楚拒绝的观点，另一方面要详细说明拒绝的理由。撰写还盘函电时，应该利用充分而合理的依据说服对方接受我方的观点或提议。在磋商过程中，注意结合谈判的利用竞争策略、软硬兼施策略、让步策略等促使对方合作。

（2）培养灵活应变的能力。

面对客户不合理的还盘要求时，我方应该不卑不亢、据理力争，同时灵活地为对方提供可选择的方案，让客户感受到我方诚恳的态度。

（3）培养良好的抗压能力。

磋商阶段可能需要经历多轮还盘才能达成合作，所以在此过程中应培养良好的抗压能力，把压力转变为动力，积极打破僵局、促成交易。

课后习题

（一）单项选择

（1）While appreciating the good quality of your products, we are sorry to say that your price appears to be（　　）.

　　A. in the high level　　　　　　　　B. at the high end
　　C. of the high standard　　　　　　D. on the high side

（2）As we have quoted you rock-bottom price, we regret that we are unable to（　　）any counter-offer.

　　A. accepting　　B. entertain　　C. receiving　　D. take

（3）This is our best price,（　　）which we have concluded many orders with other buyers in your city.

　　A. on　　B. for　　C. by　　D. at

（4）（　　）reply, we would like to say that it is very difficult for us to do business on your terms.

　　A. To　　B. In　　C. For　　D. On

（5）Please inform us（　　）the supply and demand situation in your country.

　　A. to　　B. of　　C. with　　D. in

（6）This kind of gloves is made of genuine leather（　　）high quality.

　　A. by　　B. in　　C. of　　D. on

（7）To（　　）in a market with established brands, your product must be very（　　）, both in quality and in price.

　　A. compete, competition　　　　　B. competitive, compete
　　C. compete, competitive　　　　　D. competitive, competition

(8) Material of similar products is easily obtainable (   ) a much lower price.

A. at	B. on	C. from	D. for

(9) Because of the weak market, we have to decrease our price (   ) 5%.

A. with	B. to	C. by	D. for

(10) We shall make a reduction (   ) our price if you increase the quantity (   ) 1,000 pieces.

A. on, to	B. at, to	C. on, for	D. to, to

(二) 汉译英

(1) 很遗憾,贵方价格过高,我方难以接受。

(2) 贵公司产品的价格比同类产品高 10%～15%。

(3) 如果你方能给我们一个 5% 的折扣的话,我们肯定能订购 5000 打 80 号产品。

(4) 很遗憾地告诉您,我司不能提供这么大的折扣。

(5) 为了建立我们长期互利的业务关系,如果你方能把每款产品的订购数量增加到 1300 件,我们决定破例给你 3% 的折扣。

(三) 选择填空

(1) Thank you for (   ) for 1,000 sets of Butterfly Brand sewing machines at $60 per set CIF London.

However, we regret to inform you that our end-users here find your price (   ) and out of line with the prevailing market level. As you know, the price of sewing machines has (   ) since last year. You may be aware that some dealers are lowering their prices. Under these circumstances, it is impossible for us to accept your price. If you (   ) your price by 5%, we may proceed with this transaction.

We are making this (   ) based on the long-standing business relationship between us. As the market is declining, we hope you will consider our counteroffer.

We would appreciate a speedy response.

A. reduce

B. counteroffer

C. your offer

D. declined

E. on the high side

(2) We are sorry to learn from your letter of July 30th, 2020 that you find our prices (   ). We do our best to keep our price (   ) without sacrificing quality. Considering the quality of the canned mushroom offered, we do not feel that the price we quoted is at all excessive. However, since it is the first time we do business, we have decided to offer you a (   ) of 4%. We make this allowance because we should like to start business with you, but we must stress that it is the (   ) we can go. We hope this (   ) will now enable you to place an order.

A. as low as possible

B. special discount

C. revised offer

D. too high

E. furthest

(四)实训操作

4~5 名同学为一组,其中 1 名同学扮演进口商,其他同学扮演出口商。

扮演进口商的同学针对任务二中其选出的发盘做出还盘,扮演出口商的同学针对进口商的还盘分别撰写还盘函。

扮演进口商的同学选出写得最好的一封还盘函并说明原因。

任务四 接受与签订合同

Task Four: Acceptance and Signing Contract

任务导入

> 经过多次讨价还价,客户 Martin Albert 于 2021 年 11 月 27 日写信接受了张爱华提出的交易条件。张爱华根据交易磋商的结果,制定了外贸销售合同,并写信请客户签署合同,确认订单。

外贸业务指引

接受是指受盘人无条件同意发盘(或还盘)的内容,并愿意签订合同的一种口头或书面的表示。接受可由买方表示,也可由卖方发出,但必须由合法的受盘人发出,而且接受表示须在发盘有效期内送达发盘人。无论是卖方还是买方表示接受,都应在接受函里将达成一致的重要交易条件,如产品、价格、数量、包装、发货期、支付方式等再次进行确认,避免引起后续纠纷。

一、接受函

发件人(From)	Albert@yaoo.com
收件人(To)	Zhangaihua@mail.hengxin.com
主题(Subject)	Acceptance for BP005,BP011,BP020
时间(Time)	Nov. 27th, 2021
附件(Attachment)	

Dear Ms. Zhang,

We acknowledged your counter-offer of Nov. 25th. After careful consideration, we decide to accept paying by 100% irrevocable documentary L/C at sight in seller's favor. Please send us the signed S/C with your company chop covering the following points:

1. Article: BP005 Glowing Bath Toy.
   Pattern: whale.
   Price: US$ 3.3/pc, CIF Bangkok.
   Quantity: 1,300 pcs.
   Packing: 1 piece in a box, 65 boxes in a carton.

2. Article: BP011 Rainbow Unicorn Night Light.
   Pattern: unicorn.
   Price: US$ 6.2/pc, CIF Bangkok.
   Quantity: 1,300 pcs.
   Packing: 1 piece in a box, 20 boxes in a carton.

3. Article: BP020 Sleepy Chick.
   Pattern: chick.
   Price: US$ 16.6/pc, CIF Bangkok.
   Quantity: 1,300 pcs.
   Packing: 1 piece in a box, 20 boxes in a carton.

Terms of Payment: 100% irrevocable documentary L/C at sight in seller's favor.
Date of Shipment: within one month after receipt of the L/C.

Please don't forget that bank details should be marked in the S/C for us to open the L/C.

Best regards!

Martin Albert
Purchasing Manager

1. 常用词汇

acknowledge	确认收到
S/C (sales contract)	销售合同
sign	签(名),署(名),签字,签署
chop	(公司)图章

2. 常用句型

(1) After careful consideration, we decide to accept paying by 100% irrevocable documentary L/C at sight in seller's favor.

(2) Please send us the signed S/C with your company chop covering the following points.

(3) Please don't forget that bank details should be marked in the S/C for us to open the L/C.

外贸业务指引

交易一旦达成,我们最好能以书面合同的形式将各种交易条件确定下来。在国际贸易中,书面合同不仅是买卖双方建立合同关系的依据,也是买卖双方履行合同的依据以及合同生效的依据。

二、签订合同

发件人(From)	Zhangaihua@mail.hengxin.com
收件人(To)	Albert@yaoo.com
主题(Subject)	S/C No. HXEP086 for 3,600 pcs of night lights
时间(Time)	Nov. 28th, 2021
附件(Attachment)	Sales Contract No. HXEP086

Dear Mr. Albert,

We are glad to have been able to conclude this initial transaction with you. Enclosed please find our Sales Contract No. HXEP086 in duplicate for 3,600 pcs of night lights. Please countersign and return one copy for our file.

Of course, we will execute the order strictly conforming to the S/C stipulations.

Looking forward to receiving your future enquiries and orders.

Best regards!

Aihua Zhang
Sales Manager
Guangzhou Hengxin Lighting Technology Co., Ltd.
24 Zhannan Road, Yuexiu District, Guangzhou, P. R. China 510010
Email: Zhangaihua@mail.hengxin.com
Tel: 0086-020-86668420
Fax: 0086-020-86668421

1. 常用词汇

conclude	达成(协议)
in duplicate	一式二份

countersign	副署,会签(文件)
for our file	供我方存档
execute	执行
conforming to	符合,遵循
stipulation	条款,约定(规定)的条件

2. 常用句型

(1) We are glad to have been able to conclude this initial transaction with you.

(2) Enclosed please find our Sales Contract No. HXEP086 in duplicate for 3,600 pcs of night lights.

(3) Please countersign and return one copy for our file.

(4) Of course, we will execute the order strictly conforming to the S/C stipulations.

(5) Looking forward to receiving your future enquiries and orders.

思政园地

(1) 培养严谨认真的做事态度,起草或审查好合同内容。

在合同签订环节,应认真起草合同或对合同进行仔细审查,确认无误后双方签字。培养严谨认真的做事态度有利于业务顺利进行,能让客户获得良好的合作体验,并有助于双方建立长远的合作关系。

(2) 树立正确的法律观念,培养良好的契约精神。

达成交易有多种具体的书面形式,包括订单、确认书、合同等,其中合同形式是有力的法律依据。尤其在与客户第一次合作时,我们应提升法治素养,运用法律武器维护好双方的合法权益,履行好约定的义务,并推动交易顺利完成。

课后习题

(一) 单项选择

(1) We enclosed our Purchase Confirmation No. 4848 (　　) duplicate.

    A. in　　　　　　B. for　　　　　　C. with　　　　　　D. through

(2) Please (　　) one copy of Purchase Confirmation completed (　　) your countersignature.

    A. send, with　　B. fill, on　　C. fill, with　　D. return, with

(3) We are not in a position to promise a firm offer, as the goods are (　　).

    A. without stock　　　　　　B. outside in stock

    C. out of stock　　　　　　D. out stock

(4) Please countersign the S/C and return one copy (　　) our record.

    A. for　　　　　　B. in　　　　　　C. on　　　　　　D. to

(5) The stocks are running (　　).

    A. low　　　　　　B. stop　　　　　　C. little　　　　　　D. limited

(6)In most cases, goods are ordered on (   ) order forms.

A. print B. printing C. to print D. printed

(7)We find your terms (   ) and now send you our order for 10 SM combines.

A. fitful B. suitable C. satisfied D. satisfactory

(8)Please open the covering L/C (   ) our favor.

A. at B. for C. in D. to

(9)Please supply the following items (   ) the understanding that the commission is 5% on each in Order No. 256.

A. based on B. on the basis of
C. on D. on the terms of

(10)We hope to book (   ) you a repeat order (   ) the following lines (   ) USD 230 per set CIF Bangkok.

A. from, for, at B. for, of, on
C. with, for, at D. \, with, on

(二)汉译英

(1)按你们的要求,我们随函寄去第456号销售确认书一式三份,请查收。

(2)所附上的是我们第986号销售合同一式两份,如果你方认为没问题,请签退一份供我方备案。

(3)感谢你方的合作,希望此次合作成为我们双方长期友好关系的开端。

(4)我们很高兴与贵公司完成首次订单的交易,期待双方贸易的扩大和长期的贸易关系。

(5)尽管目前市场坚挺并有上涨趋势,但为了促进交易,我们破例接受你方订单。

(三)选择填空

(1)Thank you for your fax of Sep. 20th (   ) our request for a 5% reduction in price. We are pleased to confirm (   ) with you on the terms and conditions stated below.

Commodity: Habotai.

Art. No.: PS080.

Quantity: 30,000 yards.

Unit price: at USD 1.2/yd, (   ).

Packing: in rolls of 50 yards each, (   ) to an export standard carton lined with plastic sheets.

Port of loading: Shanghai.

Port of destination: New York.

Time of shipment: in three equal monthly lots beginning from Oct. 2013.

Other terms remain unchanged.

We'll instruct our bank to open the covering L/C upon our (   ) your confirmation and look forward to your early reply.

A. placing an order

B. CIF New York

C. satisfying

D. receipt of

E. 10 rolls

(2) We confirm our (   ) to your order No. PP238 you emailed us this morning for the five kinds of printing paper. And we welcome you as one of our customers.

We are pleased to send you in the attached file the (   ) No. PP080315 for your (   ). Please (   ) it and return it to us for our file. And please open your L/C by the end of this month. Shipment will be made upon our receipt of your L/C.

Your cooperation is highly (   ). We assure you of our best service and look forward to receiving more orders from you.

A. Sales Confirmation

B. acceptance

C. appreciated

D. countersign

E. e-signature

(四)实训操作

4~5 名同学为一组,其中 1 名同学扮演进口商,其他同学扮演出口商。

扮演进口商的同学针对任务三实训操作中出口商的还盘,撰写一封接受函。

扮演出口商的同学针对接受函,分别撰写签订合同的相关信函。

项目四　合同的履行

Project Four: Execution of Contract

学习目标

【思政目标】

培养学生的工作责任感以及良好的环保意识；

培养学生遵循诚实信用原则，恪守职业道德；

培养学生良好的风险意识，确保支付和货物运输安全；

培养学生良好的时间观念与契约精神，培养学生爱岗敬业、忠于职守的工匠精神。

【知识目标】

掌握包装、支付、装运及保险相关的常用英文词汇及句型；

掌握与客户沟通包装细节相关信函的内容和写作方法；

掌握催开、修改信用证，要求接受不符点，要求付款相关信函的内容和写作方法；

掌握与客户沟通装运事项及装船通知相关信函的内容和写作方法；

掌握与客户沟通投保事项相关信函的内容和写作方法。

【能力目标】

能够根据实际情况撰写描述产品包装情况的相关信函；

能够撰写催证函、改证函，及要求客户接受不符点和要求客户付款的信函；

能够在发货前根据生产和租船情况撰写装运相关信函，在发货后撰写装运通知；

能够撰写与客户讨论保险事项的相关信函。

任务一　包装

Task One: Packing

任务导入

除了价格与支付方式之外,在签订合同之前,张爱华就包装问题也与客户进行了沟通(为了便于学习相关内容,所以将包装相关信函统一放在此处讲解)。并且,在签订合同后,张爱华对合同又进行了复核,发现合同当中的包装条款写得不太具体、明确,为了避免后续的麻烦,张爱华修订了合同,并写信告知客户,请客户就补充条款再次签字盖章。

外贸业务指引

包装是货物的重要组成部分,也是国际贸易业务的重要交易条件之一。进出口双方在进行交易磋商的过程中,应以书面形式对包装相关问题进行详细规定,通常涉及以下几个方面:包装方式、包装材料、唛头和包装费用等。如果客户对包装有特殊要求,应提供准确的最终包装设计稿给客户确认。

一、进口商提出包装要求

发件人(From)	Albert@yaoo.com
收件人(To)	Zhangaihua@mail.hengxin.com
主题(Subject)	Packing Requirements of BP005,BP011,BP020
时间(Time)	Nov. 25th, 2021
附件(Attachment)	

Dear Ms. Zhang,

Thank you for your email of Nov. 24th. As regards the packing of our ordered goods, we suggest they should be wrapped in polythene wrappers and packed in cardboard boxes padded with foam plastic.
BP005: 1 piece to a box, 65 boxes to a wooden case.
BP011, BP020: 1 piece to a box, 20 boxes to a wooden case.

In addition, the shipping mark is at your discretion.

Please give careful consideration to our proposal. Looking forward to receiving your early reply.

Best regards!

Martin Albert
Purchasing Manager

1. 常用词汇

packing	包装,包装材料
as regards	关于,至于
wrap	用……包裹(或包扎、覆盖等)
polythene	聚乙烯
wrapper	包装材料,包装纸,包装塑料
cardboard	硬纸板,卡纸板
pad	(用软材料)填充,覆盖,保护
foam	泡沫
wooden case	木箱,木盆
in addition	另外,此外
shipping mark	运输标志,唛头
discretion	自行决定的自由,自行决定权

2. 常用句型

(1) As regards the packing of our ordered goods, we suggest they should be wrapped in polythene wrappers and packed in cardboard boxes padded with foam plastic.

(2) The shipping mark is at your discretion.

(3) Please give careful consideration to our proposal.

二、出口商推荐新型包装

发件人(From)	Zhangaihua@mail.hengxin.com
收件人(To)	Albert@yaoo.com
主题(Subject)	Re: Packing Requirements of BP005, BP011, BP020
时间(Time)	Nov. 25th, 2021
附件(Attachment)	

外贸英语函电

Dear Mr. Albert,

Thank you for your email of Nov. 25th presenting demands for the packing of the night lights.

As to the outer packing, we could use wooden cases if you think it's better. But our improved outer packing with cartons for night lights has been widely accepted by our regular clients. Each of the night lights is to be wrapped in polythene wrapper and every carton is to be lined with oilcloth, which could well protect the contents from moisture. Besides, cartons are less expensive, lighter to carry and cost lower freight. So, we suggest you accept our carton packing.

Please advise us of your comment. Looking forward to your early reply.

Best regards!

Aihua Zhang
Sales Manager
Guangzhou Hengxin Lighting Technology Co., Ltd.
24 Zhannan Road, Yuexiu District, Guangzhou, P. R. China 510010
Email: Zhangaihua@mail.hengxin.com
Tel: 0086-020-86668420
Fax: 0086-020-86668421
Mobile: 13677885566
https://www.hengxin.com

1. 常用词汇

as to	关于,至于
line	(用……)做衬里
oilcloth	油布
moisture	潮气,水分
freight	运费

2. 常用句型

(1) But our improved outer packing with cartons for night lights has been widely accepted by our regular clients.

(2) Each of the night lights is to be wrapped in polythene wrapper and every carton is to be lined with oilcloth, which could well protect the contents from moisture.

(3) Besides, cartons are less expensive, lighter to carry and cost lower freight.

三、出口商说明包装详情

发件人(From)	Zhangaihua@mail.hengxin.com
收件人(To)	Albert@yaoo.com
主题(Subject)	Packing Details of BP005，BP011，BP020
时间(Time)	Nov. 26th, 2021
附件(Attachment)	

Dear Mr. Albert,

Thank you for accepting our proposal on packing. We are pleased to state the details as follows.

BP005: 1 piece to a polybag, 1 polybag to a cardboard box, 65 boxes to a carton lined with oilcloth. The carton's dimension is 53 cm long, 32 cm wide and 23 cm high with a volume of about 0.039 cubic meter. The gross weight is 4.25 kg, while the net weight is 3.25 kg.

BP011, BP020: 1 piece to a polybag, 1 polybag to a cardboard box, 20 boxes to a carton lined with oilcloth. The carton's dimension is 53 cm long, 32 cm wide and 23 cm high with a volume of about 0.039 cubic meter. The gross weight is 10 kg, while the net weight is 9 kg.

As regards the shipping mark outside the carton, the initials of your company will be marked in a diamond, under which the port of destination and our order number should be stenciled.

If you have any special preference in this respect, please let us know and we will meet you to the best of our ability.

We thank you in advance for your early reply.

Best regards!

Aihua Zhang
Sales Manager
Guangzhou Hengxin Lighting Technology Co., Ltd.
24 Zhannan Road, Yuexiu District, Guangzhou, P. R. China 510010
Email: Zhangaihua@mail.hengxin.com
Tel: 0086-020-86668420
Fax: 0086-020-86668421
Mobile: 13677885566
https://www.hengxin.com

1. 常用词汇

state	陈述,说明,声明
polybag	塑料袋
dimension	尺寸
volume	体积,容积,容量
cubic meter	立方米
gross weight	毛重
net weight	净重
initial	(名字的)首字母
diamond	菱形
destination	目的地,终点
stencil	用模板印制

2. 常用句型

(1) The carton's dimension is 53 cm long, 32 cm wide and 23 cm high with a volume of about 0.039 cubic meter. The gross weight is 4.25 kg, while the net weight is 3.25 kg.

(2) As regards the shipping mark outside the carton, the initials of your company will be marked in a diamond, under which the port of destination and our order number should be stenciled.

(3) If you have any special preference in this respect, please let us know and we will meet you to the best of our ability.

外贸业务指引

签订合同后,在大批量生产货物之前,我们最好就包装细节再次和客户进行确认,如果有什么问题则可以及时更改,以免造成损失。

四、请进口商确认包装细节

发件人(From)	Zhangaihua@mail.hengxin.com
收件人(To)	Albert@yaoo.com
主题(Subject)	S/C No. HXEP086 Packing Clause Confirmation
时间(Time)	Dec. 24th, 2021
附件(Attachment)	

Dear Mr. Albert,

We are pleased to inform you that we have got the raw materials ready and will produce the night lights you ordered next week. In order to avoid possible future troubles, please confirm again whether there is any need to revise or supplement the packing clause in S/C No. HXEP086.

On the outer packing, except the shipping mark, the gross weight, net weight and tare, and indicative marks like THIS SIDE UP, GUARD AGAINST DAMP, etc. should also be stenciled.

We will arrange shipment next month and trust you will find the packing satisfactory and the goods in good condition after receiving the consignment.

Best regards!

Aihua Zhang
Sales Manager
Guangzhou Hengxin Lighting Technology Co., Ltd.
24 Zhannan Road, Yuexiu District, Guangzhou, P. R. China 510010
Email：Zhangaihua@mail.hengxin.com
Tel：0086-020-86668420
Fax：0086-020-86668421
Mobile：13677885566
https://www.hengxin.com

1. 常用词汇

clause	（法律文件等的）条款
supplement	增补，补充
tare	包装重量
indicative mark	指示性标志
this side up	此面朝上
guard against damp	防潮
consignment	装运的货物，运送物

2. 常用句型

(1) In order to avoid possible future troubles, please confirm again whether there is any need to revise or supplement the packing clause in S/C No. HXEP086.

(2) On the outer packing, except the shipping mark, the gross weight, net weight and tare, and indicative marks like THIS SIDE UP, GUARD AGAINST DAMP, etc. should also be stenciled.

(3) We will arrange shipment next month and trust you will find the packing satisfactory and the goods in good condition after receiving the consignment.

拓展阅读

包装相关常见英文表达

1. 常用包装物

case	箱	carton	纸箱
corrugated carton	瓦楞纸箱	wooden case	木箱
crate	板条箱	wooden crate	木条箱
cardboard box	纸板盒	plywood case	胶合板箱
3-ply plywood case	三层夹板箱	wooden box	木盒
bag(sack)	袋	gunny bag/jute bag	麻袋
nylon bag	尼龙袋	poly bag	塑料袋
poly-woven bag	塑料编织袋	3-ply craft paper bag	三层牛皮纸袋
jumbo bag	特大袋	drum	桶
wooden cask	木桶	barrel	桶
straw bale	草包	press packed bale	紧压包
can	罐	tin	听
basket	笼(篓、篮)	bamboo basket	竹笼(篓、篮、筐)
wicker basket	柳条筐	container	集装箱
pallet	托盘		

2. 常用的指示性与警告性标志

Handle with care	小心搬运	This side up	此面朝上
Not to be thrown down	请勿抛掷	Not to be laid flat	请勿平放
No hooks	请勿用钩	Keep upright	勿倒置
Keep out of the direct sun	避免日光直射	Guard against damp	防潮
Keep cool	保持冷藏	Keep away from cold	请勿受冷
Keep away from heat	请勿受热	Keep dry	防湿
Keep in a dry place	在干燥处保管	Keep in a cool place	在冷处保管
Keep away from boilers	远离锅炉	Perishable goods	易腐物品
Fragile	易碎品	Corrosive	腐蚀性物品

Dangerous goods	危险品	Explosive	爆炸品
Inflammable	易燃品	Poison	有毒物品
Poison gas	毒气	Radioactive	放射性物品

思政园地

(1)培养学生的工作责任感。

注重产品的包装问题,及时通过函电与客户进行协商和确认。尤其当客户对产品有特殊的包装要求时,应该明确买卖双方的包装责任,包括包装材料、包装方式、包装标志、包装费用等方面。提升工作责任感,履行好包装责任,保障产品在运输、销售过程中呈现出更好的效果。

(2)培养学生的环保意识,注意适度包装。

良好的包装有利于方便产品运输以及提高销量,但是过度的包装会造成浪费或环境污染。因此,要树立良好的环保意识,在包装的函电协商中注意采用合适的包装材料和包装方式,以利于可持续发展。

课后习题

(一)单项选择

(1) All the canned fruits and meat are to be packed (　　) cartons.
A. in　　　　　　B. at　　　　　　C. of　　　　　　D. with

(2) Please see to it that the packing is suitable (　　) a long sea voyage.
A. of　　　　　　B. for　　　　　　C. in　　　　　　D. with

(3) Please mark the outer packing (　　) our initials SCC (　　) a diamond, under which the port of destination and our order number should be stenciled.
A. with, at　　　B. with, in　　　C. of, at　　　　D. of, in

(4) Our Trip Scissors are packed in boxes (　　) 1 dozen each, 100 boxes (　　) a carton lined with waterproof paper.
A. of, of　　　　B. in, in　　　　C. in, of　　　　D. of, in

(5) The wooden case should be not only seaworthy but also strong enough to protect the goods (　　) damage.
A. of　　　　　　B. to　　　　　　C. from　　　　　D. in

(6) The goods had been (　　) before they were delivered to our customers.
A. pack　　　　　B. repacked　　　C. package　　　　D. packing

(7) All the shirts are to be packed in poly-bags of one piece (　　).
A. some　　　　　B. each　　　　　C. every　　　　　D. any

(8) The boxes are to be (　　) with the initials of our company in a diamond as usual.

A. mark   B. marks   C. marked   D. marking

(9) Please line the wooden cases (　　) waterproof material so that the goods can be protected (　　) moisture.

A. with, with   B. with, against

C. against, against   D. against, with

(10) Please pack our men's shirts (　　) cartons (　　) 50 dozen each.

A. in, in   B. in, of

C. of, of   D. of, in

(二) 汉译英

(1) 请用纸盒包装男式衬衫,每件装一盒,一百盒装一纸箱,箱外打两道塑料带。

(2) 为方便搬运和节省运费,今后我们将采用纸箱包装代替原来的木箱包装。

(3) 包装必须牢固,易于搬运,且适合远洋运输。

(4) 这些纸板箱用塑料衬里,防潮性能好。

(5) 我们将按照贵方指令刷唛。

(三) 选择填空

(1) We are glad to inform you of the (　　) details for our Printed Shirting as follows.

The Printed Shirting are first (　　) bales of 50 meters each, and then put into a plastic bag, five bags to a (　　) lined with polythene sheets. On the outer packing, we mark the (　　) NYT of the consignee in a triangle, under which the port of destination New York and the contract number are (　　). In addition, indicative mark like "KEEP DRY" is printed as well.

We look forward to your confirmation soon.

A. packed in

B. packing and marking

C. stenciled

D. carton

E. initials

(2) We refer to our order No. 6054 for 200 cardboard cartons of beer glasses to be shipped during May. As the goods are highly (　　), we advise to pack the goods according to our instructions to (　　) damage in transit.

Please pack the goods half dozen in a box, 10 boxes (　　) a carton, and two cartons in a wooden case. The boxes are to be (　　) with foamed plastics. Apart from this, we hope the (　　) will be attractive and helpful to sales while the outer packing strong enough to withstand rough handling and the sea transportation.

We hope our goods will arrive in perfect condition.

A. prevent

B. padded

C. fragile

D. inner packing

E. in

（四）实训操作

4~5 名同学为一组，其中 1 名同学扮演进口商，其他同学扮演出口商。

扮演出口商的同学结合之前实训操作中商品的具体情况，分别撰写信函向进口商说明自己公司包装的详细情况。

扮演进口商的同学选出最好的一封介绍包装的信函并说明原因。

任务二 支付

Task Two: Payment

任务导入

张爱华于 2021 年 11 月 28 日和客户签订了外贸销售合同，合同中规定支付方式为以卖方为受益人的不可撤销即期信用证。但是已经过去半个多月了，她仍然没有收到客户开过来的信用证，于是张爱华于 2021 年 12 月 16 日写信催促客户开立信用证。收到信用证后，经审核，她发现信用证上存在一些与合同不一致的条款，于是，张爱华又于 2021 年 12 月 20 日写信请客户修改信用证。

外贸业务指引

催证指出口商通知或催促国外进口商按照合同规定迅速通过银行开立信用证，以便出口商能将货物及时装运。当合同中规定以信用证为支付方式且装运期临近时，若进口方未按约定时间开立信用证，出口方为避免耽误装船，应迅速发出催证函。

在一般情况下，进口商至少应在货物装运期前 15 天将信用证开到出口商手中。对于资信情况不是很明确的新客户，原则上应坚持让对方在装运期前 30 天或 45 天甚至更长的期限内开立信用证，并且应配合生产加工期限和客户的要求灵活掌握信用证的开证日期。在实际业务中，国外客户在遇到市场行情变化或缺乏资金的情况下，往往拖延开证，因此，出口商应及时检查并敦促进口商开证。

一、催证函(1)

发件人(From)	Zhangaihua@mail.hengxin.com
收件人(To)	Albert@yaoo.com
主题(Subject)	Our S/C No. HXEP086 for 3,600 pcs of Night Lights
时间(Time)	Dec. 16th, 2021
附件(Attachment)	

Dear Mr. Albert,

With reference to the 3,600 pcs of night lights under S/C No. HXEP086, we wish to draw your attention to the fact that the date of delivery is approaching, but up to now we have not received the covering L/C. Please do your best to expedite its establishment, so that we may ship the order within the prescribed time.

In order to avoid subsequent amendments, please ensure that the L/C stipulations are in conformity with those in the S/C.

We hope to receive your favorable reply soon.

Best regards!

Aihua Zhang
Sales Manager
Guangzhou Hengxin Lighting Technology Co., Ltd.
24 Zhannan Road, Yuexiu District, Guangzhou, P. R. China 510010
Email：Zhangaihua@mail.hengxin.com
Tel：0086-020-86668420
Fax：0086-020-86668421
Mobile：13677885566
https://www.hengxin.com

1. 常用词汇

draw your attention	提醒你方注意
approach	靠近,临近
up to now	至今,到现在为止
do your best	尽你所能
expedite	加快,促进,发出
prescribed	规定的
subsequent	后来的,随后的
amendment	修改
in conformity with	与……相符,符合

2. 常用句型

(1) With reference to the 3,600 pcs of night lights under S/C No. HXEP086, we wish to draw your attention to the fact that the date of delivery is approaching, but up to now we have not received the covering L/C.

(2) Please do your best to expedite its establishment, so that we may ship the order within the prescribed time.

(3) In order to avoid subsequent amendments, please ensure that the L/C stipulations are

in conformity with those in the S/C.

二、催证函(2)

发件人(From)	Zhangaihua@mail.hengxin.com
收件人(To)	Albert@yaoo.com
主题(Subject)	Our S/C No. HXEP086 for 3,600 pcs of Night Lights
时间(Time)	Dec. 16th, 2021
附件(Attachment)	

Dear Mr. Albert,

Referring to the 3,600 pcs of night lights under S/C No. HXEP086, we write to inform you that the relative L/C should have reached us before the end of last week as contracted. But so far, we regret having received neither the required credit nor any further information from you even though we sent you a fax one week ago pressing you for the establishment of the L/C.

Please expedite and inform us of the establishment of an L/C so that we can effect shipment within the stipulated time. In order to avoid subsequent possible amendments, please see to it that the L/C stipulations are in exact accordance with the terms of the S/C.

We are expecting your L/C coming soon and thanks for your cooperation.

Best regards!

Aihua Zhang
Sales Manager
Guangzhou Hengxin Lighting Technology Co., Ltd.
24 Zhannan Road, Yuexiu District, Guangzhou, P. R. China 510010
Email: Zhangaihua@mail.hengxin.com
Tel: 0086-020-86668420
Fax: 0086-020-86668421
Mobile: 13677885566
https://www.hengxin.com

1. 常用词汇

referring to	关于
relative	相关联的
fax	传真

press	催促，敦促，逼迫
effect	使发生，实现，引起
stipulated	规定的
see to it	务必要
in accordance with	依照，与……一致

2. 常用句型

（1）We write to inform you that the relative L/C should have reached us before the end of last week as contracted.

（2）But so far, we regret having received neither the required credit nor any further information from you even though we sent you a fax two weeks ago pressing you for the establishment of the L/C.

（3）We are expecting your L/C coming soon and thanks for your cooperation.

- 请比较以上2封催证函，哪一封比较好呢？

营销知识链接

无论客户是无意还是故意迟开信用证，我们在催促客户开立信用证时一般都会给出一个理由，或者是我们的货已经准备好了，或者是发货期马上就要到了，或者是合同中规定的开证日期已经到了。很显然，在这几个理由当中，最后一个理由对客户来说最有说服力，因为如果超过合同规定的时间他仍不开证，将意味着他违约了。而如果客户是故意的，前两个理由对他来说将毫无说服力，因为不开信用证不会给他带来任何损失。由此可见，催开信用证不仅仅是写封信这么简单，要想真正达到我们的目的，就要对所有可能的风险进行预判，并将防范措施写进外贸销售合同里，以对客户形成制约。

外贸业务指引

收到信用证，我们需要在第一时间审证，并通知客户具体需要修改的地方。即使全部接受，没有地方需要修改，我们也需要给客户一个确认的答复。一般情况下，客户会先提供一个草稿件给我们确认，然后再请银行出具正本的信用证，这样能最大限度地避免改证的费用和麻烦。

三、改证函（1）

发件人（From）	Zhangaihua@mail.hengxin.com
收件人（To）	Albert@yaoo.com
主题（Subject）	Amendment to Your L/C No. ABL-OP529
时间（Time）	Dec. 20th, 2021
附件（Attachment）	

Dear Mr. Albert,

Your Letter of Credit No. ABL-OP529 covering 3,600 pcs of night lights has been received today.

Upon checking the L/C with the contract, we regret to find that it contains some discrepancies which please amend as follows:

1. The contract number should be "HXEP086" instead of "HXEP860".

2. "Shipment should be effected in a single lot not later than December 31, 2021" should be amended to "shipment should be made in a single lot within January 2022".

3. Since direct steamers from here to your port are few, please amend the L/C to read "transshipment allowed".

4. The place of expiry should be "in China" instead of "in Thailand".

As the goods have been ready for shipment for quite some time, please make the amendments to the L/C as soon as possible so that we can effect shipment in time.

Looking forward to your early amendment for the relevant L/C.

Best regards!

Aihua Zhang
Sales Manager
Guangzhou Hengxin Lighting Technology Co., Ltd.
24 Zhannan Road, Yuexiu District, Guangzhou, P. R. China 510010
Email: Zhangaihua@mail.hengxin.com
Tel: 0086-020-86668420
Fax: 0086-020-86668421
Mobile: 13677885566
https://www.hengxin.com

1. 常用词汇

amendment	修改,改正
discrepancy	不符,矛盾,相差
amend	修改,改正
lot	(一)组,群,批,套
steamer	轮船
read	写成,写着

transshipment	转运
expiry	（文件、协议等的）满期，届期，到期
relevant	相关的

2. 常用句型

(1) Upon checking the L/C with the contract, we regret to find that it contains some discrepancies which please amend as follows.

(2) "Shipment should be effected in a single lot not later than December 31, 2021" should be amended to "shipment should be made in a single lot within January 2022".

(3) Since direct steamers from here to your port are few, please amend the L/C to read "transshipment allowed".

(4) The place of expiry should be "in China" instead of "in Thailand".

(5) As the goods have been ready for shipment for quite some time, please make the amendments to the L/C as soon as possible so that we can effect shipment in time.

四、改证函(2)

发件人(From)	Zhangaihua@mail.hengxin.com
收件人(To)	Albert@yaoo.com
主题(Subject)	Amendment to Your L/C No. ABL-OP529
时间(Time)	Dec. 20th, 2021
附件(Attachment)	

Dear Mr. Albert,

Thank you for your L/C No. ABL-OP529 issued by Krungthai Bank Public Company Limited dated Dec. 18th, 2021. On perusal, we found some discrepancies unacceptable to us. Please amend the credit as follows:

1) 40 FORM OF DOC. CREDIT

Please amend "revocable" to "irrevocable". A credit is irrevocable even if there is no indication to that effect in accordance with *UCP 600*.

2) 31D DATE AND PLACE

The expiry place should be "in China" as contracted. While please change the negotiating bank "KRUNGTHAI BANK PUBLIC COMPANY LIMITED BANGKOK BRANCH" in the clause "41D AVAILABLE WITH/BY". It is inconvenient for us to negotiate in BANGKOK. You should choose a negotiating bank in China.

3) 45A DESCRIPTS. OF GOODS

The quantity of BP011 is "1300" instead of "1000".

The trade terms are "CIF BANGKOK DETAILS AS PER S/C NO. HXEP086", not "CIFC3 BANGKOK DETAILS AS PER S/C NO. HXEP086".

4) 71B DETAILS OF CHARGES

The opening fee is to be borne by the applicant according to the usual practices. So please amend to "All banking charges outside the country of issue are for the account of beneficiary".

We also regret that we could not ship the goods by December vessel only because of the delay of your L/C. Please extend the shipping date of your L/C to Jan. 30th, 2022 and validity to Feb. 15th, 2022 respectively.

Please give this letter your prompt attention and make sure that the L/C amendment advice should reach us by Dec. 25th, 2021.

Best regards!

Aihua Zhang
Sales Manager
Guangzhou Hengxin Lighting Technology Co., Ltd.
24 Zhannan Road, Yuexiu District, Guangzhou, P. R. China 510010
Email：Zhangaihua@mail.hengxin.com
Tel：0086-020-86668420
Fax：0086-020-86668421
Mobile：13677885566
https://www.hengxin.com

1. 常用词汇

Krungthai Bank Public Company Limited	泰京银行
perusal	阅读,仔细查看,仔细研究
negotiate	议付
opening fee	开证费
borne	承担,担负（bear 的过去分词）
applicant	开证申请人
beneficiary	受益人
vessel	大船,轮船
validity	（法律上的）有效,合法
respectively	分别地,依次地

2. 常用句型

(1) On perusal, we found some discrepancies unacceptable to us.

(2) Please amend "revocable" to "irrevocable".

(3) While please change the negotiating bank "KRUNGTHAI BANK PUBLIC COMPANY LIMITED BANGKOK BRANCH" in the clause "41D AVAILABLE WITH/BY".

(4) The trade terms are "CIF BANGKOK DETAILS AS PER S/C NO. HXEP086", not "CIFC3 BANGKOK DETAILS AS PER S/C NO. TF987".

(5) So please amend to "All banking charges outside the country of issue are for the account of beneficiary".

(6) We also regret that we could not ship the goods by December vessel only because of the delay of your L/C.

(7) Please extend the shipping date of your L/C to Jan. 30th, 2022 and validity to Feb. 15th, 2022 respectively.

(8) Please give this letter your prompt attention and make sure that the L/C amendment advice should reach us by Dec. 25th, 2021.

营销知识链接

通过对比以上两封改证函，可以明显看出，第二封改证函的内容更加清晰，也更便于进口商进行改证操作。我们撰写改证函的时候，尤其是需要修改的内容比较多的时候，应尽量以信用证的条款来对需要修改的内容进行编号，这样做的好处是不会遗漏任何一项。另外，在撰写改证函时，尽量一次性将需要修改的内容全部告知客户，如果需要对信用证进行展期，也要同时告知客户，不要来来回回多次修改。

外贸业务指引

信用证在交单的时候，经常会有不符点产生。因为信用证一般在生产前开立，而生产过程中可能会出现各种变数，比如客户要改一些包装上的设计，或者航运出了某些问题，但这些变数并非大到非修改信用证不可的地步。在这种情况下，如果不是特别严重的问题，只要得到客户的确认，银行是可以继续偿付的。所以，我们需要在交单给银行的同时，或者在银行指出不符点的情况下，请客户确认并接受不符点。

五、请客户接受信用证不符点

发件人(From)	Zhangaihua@mail.hengxin.com
收件人(To)	Albert@yaoo.com
主题(Subject)	Pls Accept Discrepancies of L/C No. ABL-OP529
时间(Time)	Feb. 10th, 2022
附件(Attachment)	

Dear Mr. Albert,

Please find the discrepancies below mentioned by our bank:

1. As to the shipping agent, we can only show "VITA International Freight Co., Ltd." in the B/L instead of "WIN Logistics Co., Ltd." which is required in your L/C.

2. The destination port was changed to Laem Chabang, not Bangkok.

The two issues above were already approved by your shipping colleague. Please help to check and give Krungthai Bank Public Company Limited your acceptation, and we could get the payment soon.

Thanks and best regards,

Aihua Zhang
Sales Manager
Guangzhou Hengxin Lighting Technology Co., Ltd.
24 Zhannan Road, Yuexiu District, Guangzhou, P. R. China 510010
Email: Zhangaihua@mail.hengxin.com
Tel: 0086-020-86668420
Fax: 0086-020-86668421
Mobile: 13677885566
https://www.hengxin.com

1. 常用词汇

shipping agent	运货代理商,装船代理处
logistics	后勤,物流
destination port	目的港
Laem Chabang	林查班(泰国港口)
colleague	同事

2. 常用句型

(1) Please find the discrepancies below mentioned by our bank.

(2) The two issues above were already approved by your shipping colleague.

(3) Please help to check and give Krungthai Bank Public Company Limited your acceptation, and we could get the payment soon.

营销知识链接

信用证交单时常见的不符点包括：①信用证过期；②信用证装运日期过期；③受益人交单过期；④运输单据不洁净；⑤运输单据类别不可接受；⑥没有"货物已装船"证明或注明"货装舱

面";⑦运费由受益人承担,但运输单据上没有"运费付讫"字样;⑧启运港、目的港或转运港与信用证的规定不符;⑨汇票上面付款人的名称、地址等不符;⑩汇票上面的出票日期不明;⑪货物短装或超装;⑫发票上面的货物描述与信用证不符;⑬发票的抬头人的名称、地址等与信用证不符;⑭保险金额不足,保险比例与信用证不符;⑮保险单据的签发日期迟于运输单据的签发日期(不合理);⑯投保的险种与信用证不符;⑰各种单据的类别与信用证不符;⑱各种单据中的币别不一致;⑲汇票、发票或保险单据金额的大小写不一致;⑳汇票、运输单据和保险单据的背书错误或应有但没有背书;㉑单据没有必要签字或有效印章;㉒单据的份数与信用证不一致;㉓各种单据上的唛头不一致;㉔各种单据上面的货物数量和重量描述不一致。所以,在履行信用证结算的合同时,我们一定要慎重再慎重,认真核对所有单据,力求不要出现以上不符点,尤其是与客户第一次合作时。

外贸业务指引

　　由于信用证操作起来比较复杂,成本也较高,很多企业尤其是小企业一般不太愿意用信用证来结算。对于一些金额较小的订单,也不太有必要使用信用证。所以,外贸业务中最常见的付款方式其实是电汇。如果合同的付款方式是后 T/T,出货后,要第一时间提交相关单据给客户并催款,确保货款能早日收到。即使是用信用证或 D/P 之类的付款方式,单据需要提交给银行而不是客户,一般也应该给客户一份单据供其参考,并告知货已经出运。

六、提醒客户付尾款

发件人(From)	Zhangaihua@mail.hengxin.com
收件人(To)	Albert@yaoo.com
主题(Subject)	Shipping Docs and Copy of B/L
时间(Time)	Jan. 21st, 2022
附件(Attachment)	

Dear Mr. Albert,

All the night lights you ordered have been shipped last Wednesday. Enclosed you can find the invoice, packing list and copy of B/L. The ETA is Jan. 29th, to Kantang.

Please help to settle the balance USD 23,751 to our bank account soon.

Thanks and best regards,

Aihua Zhang

```
Sales Manager
Guangzhou Hengxin Lighting Technology Co.，Ltd.
24 Zhannan Road，Yuexiu District，Guangzhou，P. R. China 510010
Email：Zhangaihua@mail.hengxin.com
Tel：0086-020-86668420
Fax：0086-020-86668421
Mobile：13677885566
https://www.hengxin.com
```

1. 常用词汇

invoice	发票
packing list	装箱单
ETA	预计到达时间
Kantang	干当(泰国港口)
settle	付清(欠款)，结算，结账

2. 常用句型

(1) The ETA is Jan. 29th, to Kantang.

(2) Please help to settle the balance USD 23,751 to our bank account soon.

外贸业务指引

很多时候,我们已经通知客户付款,但是等了多日都不见有款项到账。这个时候就需要主动询问客户,让对方帮忙查询,或者提供银行水单。跨境汇款的审核相当严格,收款人的账户、公司名、收款银行甚至中转行的信息都需要完全准确,任何一个细节有误,甚至是拼写错误,汇款都有可能被退回或者暂时冻结。

七、请客户提供银行付款水单

发件人(From)	Zhangaihua@mail.hengxin.com
收件人(To)	Albert@yaoo.com
主题(Subject)	Payment Problem
时间(Time)	Jan. 28th, 2022
附件(Attachment)	

Dear Mr. Albert,

I'm sorry to inform you that we haven't received your payment. Could you kindly recheck it? Please also send us the bank receipt for record.

Thanks and best regards,

Aihua Zhang
Sales Manager
Guangzhou Hengxin Lighting Technology Co., Ltd.
24 Zhannan Road, Yuexiu District, Guangzhou, P. R. China 510010
Email：Zhangaihua@mail.hengxin.com
Tel：0086-020-86668420
Fax：0086-020-86668421
Mobile：13677885566
https://www.hengxin.com

1. 常用词汇

recheck	复查，再核对
bank receipt	水单，银行收据

2. 常用句型

(1) Could you kindly recheck it?
(2) Please also send us the bank receipt for record.

营销知识链接

有时候，客户提供了银行汇款水单后，就会要求我们立刻邮寄或电放提单。此时，我们一定要慎重，保险起见，还是应该等货款到账后再安排邮寄或电放提单。因为银行的水单有可能是客户伪造的，也有可能水单是真实的，但客户在填写境外汇款申请书时，故意写错一些信息，比如写错 SWIFT 号，或者公司名称跟地址对应不上等。银行收到电汇申请后，若审核发现问题，可能会联系客户退回款项。所以跨国交易要特别注意收款安全，如果款项没有到账，仅仅凭借对方的一份银行水单，是不可以提供提单的。

外贸业务指引

在收款的过程中，有时候可能会发生一些问题，比如客户少付了尾款需要补上，客户多付了尾款需要退回一部分，银行账户有问题导致款项被退回，或者客户把应该付给别人的钱错付给你等。一旦出现这类问题，需要第一时间与客户沟通，并给出处理意见。

八、与客户讨论错误的付款

发件人(From)	Zhangaihua@mail.hengxin.com
收件人(To)	Albert@yaoo.com
主题(Subject)	Payment Error
时间(Time)	Jan. 29th, 2022
附件(Attachment)	

Dear Mr. Albert,

We were informed from our bank that USD 1,000 had been added to our account by telegraphic transfer. I think the money belongs to another supplier of yours, right? Is it possible to return the money to you by check or cash when you come to China next month?

If you are encountering problems when making payment, please let me know.

Thanks and best regards,

Aihua Zhang
Sales Manager
Guangzhou Hengxin Lighting Technology Co., Ltd.
24 Zhannan Road, Yuexiu District, Guangzhou, P. R. China 510010
Email: Zhangaihua@mail.hengxin.com
Tel: 0086-020-86668420
Fax: 0086-020-86668421
Mobile: 13677885566
https://www.hengxin.com

1. 常用词汇

error	错误,差错
telegraphic transfer	电汇
check	支票(cheque)
cash	现款,现金
encounter	遭遇,遇到(尤指令人不快或困难的事)

2. 常用句型

(1) We were informed from our bank that USD 1,000 had been added to our account by telegraphic transfer.

(2) Is it possible to return the money to you by check or cash when you come to China

next month?

(3) If you are encountering problems when making payment, please let me know.

外贸业务指引

收到货款后,应该第一时间告知客户,并表示感谢。这不仅是基本的礼貌,也是为了节约客户的时间,使其不用把精力花在跟银行确认是否电汇成功上。在平时的工作中,一旦客户告知货款已经安排,就应该及时查询己方的银行账户,看是否有款项入账。

九、告知客户款项收到

发件人(From)	Zhangaihua@mail.hengxin.com
收件人(To)	Albert@yaoo.com
主题(Subject)	Balance Received with Thanks
时间(Time)	Jan. 29th, 2022
附件(Attachment)	

Dear Mr. Albert,

Have a good day! We have received the balance USD 23,751 under S/C No. HXEP086. Thank you very much for your support and trust. Hope we could expand our current business in the near future.

Thanks and best regards,

Aihua Zhang
Sales Manager
Guangzhou Hengxin Lighting Technology Co., Ltd.
24 Zhannan Road, Yuexiu District, Guangzhou, P. R. China 510010
Email: Zhangaihua@mail.hengxin.com
Tel: 0086-020-86668420
Fax: 0086-020-86668421
Mobile: 13677885566
https://www.hengxin.com

1. 常用词汇

expand   扩展,发展(业务)

2. 常用句型

(1) We have received the balance USD 23,751 under S/C No. HXEP086.

(2) Thank you very much for your support and trust.

(3) Hope we could expand our current business in the near future.

拓展阅读

支付方式相关常见英文表达

1. 汇票(bill of exchange, draft)

(1)即期汇票：sight draft, demand draft。

(2)远期汇票：time draft, usance draft。

①见票后若干天付款：at XXX days after sight。

②出票后若干天付款：at XXX days after date。

③提单签发日后若干天付款：at XXX days after the date of B/L。

④指定日期付款：on a fixed date。

2. 汇款(remittance)

(1)电汇：T/T(telegraphic transfer)。

①30% by T/T in advance and 70% balanced by D/P at sight.

②By T/T, 30% as deposit, 70% (balance)after delivery.

(2)票汇：D/D(demand draft)。

3. 托收(collection)

(1)即期付款交单：D/P at sight(documents against payment at sight)。

(2)远期付款交单：D/P after sight(documents against payment after sight)。

①D/P 60 days after sight.

②60 days D/P after sight.

(3)承兑交单：D/A(documents against acceptance)。

①D/A 60 days.

②60 days D/A.

4. 信用证(L/C, letter of credit)

(1)即期信用证：sight credit, demand credit。

(2)远期信用证：time credit, usance credit。

(3)延期付款信用证：deferred payment credit。

①货物装船后若干天付款：This credit is available by deferred payment at XXX days after the date of B/L.

②交单后若干天付款：by deferred payment at XXX days after presentation of documents。

③固定的将来日期付款：by deferred payment on (a future date) a fixed date。

(4)承兑信用证：acceptance credit。

This credit is available by acceptance of draft at XXX days after sight with XXX bank.

(5)议付信用证：negotiation credit。

(6)假远期信用证：usance letter of credit payable at sight。

(7)预支信用证:anticipatory letter of credit。
(8)可转让信用证:transferable credit。
(9)循环信用证:revolving credit。

思政园地

(1)培养学生遵循诚实信用原则,恪守职业道德。

在国际商务中,应遵循诚实信用原则,按约定的结算方式、金额、时间等完成支付手续。在不同的结算方式下,进出口双方承担不同的责任与义务。我们应该恪守职业道德,按约定办事,履行好自身有关结算的义务,并及时通过函电将结算情况反馈给对方或督促对方完成结算。

(2)树立正确的风险意识,确保外汇资金的安全。

加强对不同的结算方式的认识,并理解其特点、流程、风险等,选择合适的结算方式以降低交易的收汇风险。同时要具备正确的风险意识,对客户的资信情况做好调查,与客户保持密切函电联系并跟踪业务的收汇情况,若遇到收汇困难应该及时采取相应措施规避风险。

课后习题

(一)单项选择

(1)We have to cancel the remaining 500 pairs of your order No. 221. Kindly have the L/C (   ) accordingly.
A. amend　　　　B. to mend　　　　C. amending　　　　D. amended

(2)Our delay in payment was (   ) temporary accounting difficulties.
A. due to　　　　B. owe to　　　　C. because　　　　D. since

(3)We have (   ) at 20 days' draft for the full amount of the invoice.
A. written to you　　B. called on you　　C. sent to you by air　D. drawn on you

(4)(   ), we found there are some discrepancies in your L/C.
A. On perusal　　B. Perusal　　C. In check　　D. Check

(5)Please open an L/C immediately so that we can (   ) shipment in time.
A. made　　　　B. effect　　　　C. ship　　　　D. cover

(6)Your request for earlier payment is unacceptable to us since our liquid fund has been (   ) by some other businesses.
A. taken up　　B. brought　　C. placed　　D. tied up

(7)As there is a lack for stock of the shoes you ordered, we cannot make the shipment as scheduled. Would you please (   ) the credit to the end of June 2020?
A. expand　　　B. extend　　　C. expire　　　D. extension

(8)We have drawn a draft on you (   ) USD 1,000 (   ) the underlined commodity.
A. for, against　　　　　　　　B. for, on

C. on, against D. on, for

(9) Upon examining the L/C, we discovered that some points are not (　　) the S/C.

　　A. conform with B. conforming

　　C. in conformity with D. conformity to

(10) Taking into (　　) our long-standing business relations with you, we accept (　　) by D/P.

　　A. considering, enquiries B. consideration, invitations

　　C. considering, installment D. consideration, payment

(二) 汉译英

(1) 由于本月没有到达贵港的直达船，请将 ER325 号信用证修改为"允许转船"，而不是"不允许转船"。

(2) 请将船期延展到 10 月 30 日，有效期延展到 11 月 20 日，并尽快给我方答复。

(3) 按我方第 333 号销售合同规定，有关信用证应在 12 月 20 日前开立并抵达我方。

(4) 请帮忙核对并通知 Krungthai Bank Public Company Limited 你方接受不符点，这样我们才可以拿到货款。

(5) 我们已通知我方银行开出以你方为受益人的、金额为两万美元的、保兑的、不可撤销的信用证，该证于 10 月 1 日到期。

(三) 选择填空

(1) Thank you very much for your L/C No. BOC 2021/10/05. However, upon checking, we have found the following (　　):

①The amount of the credit (　　) CAN＄125,000 (Say Canadian Dollars One Hundred and Twenty-five Thousand Only) instead of CAN＄120,000.

②The Bill of Lading should be marked "freight prepaid" (　　) "freight to collect".

③Please (　　) Insurance Policies (or Certificates) from the credit.

④The port of destination should be Vancouver instead of Montreal.

⑤The credit should expire on December 15th, 2021 for (　　) in China instead of November 30, 2021.

We await your early amendments.

　　A. instead of

　　B. discrepancies

　　C. negotiation

　　D. should be

　　E. delete

(2) We have received your email of November 3, 2022, contents of which have been noted by us.

In compliance with your request, we have already instructed our bank to (　　) the date of shipment and (　　) of our L/C to November 30, 2022 and December 15, 2022 (　　). You can be assured that the (　　) of the L/C should reach you in due time.

Please make necessary arrangements to have the goods (　　) before or on November 30 and present the documents required by our L/C to the negotiating bank with the least possible delay.

We look forward to your shipping advice.

A. validity

B. extension advice

C. extend

D. shipped

E. respectively

(四)实训操作

4～5 名同学为一组,其中 1 名同学扮演进口商,其他同学扮演出口商。

扮演进口商的同学结合之前实训操作签订的销售合同,开立一份信用证给出口商。

扮演出口商的同学审核信用证,并撰写改证函。

任务三 保险

Task Three：Insurance

任务导入

2021 年 12 月 1 日,张爱华收到客户来信,客户要求在平安险之外,加投偷窃、提货不着险。张爱华回信与客户商讨加投该附加险的必要性,最终决定按照客户要求投保平安险、附加偷窃、提货不着险,多出的保费由客户承担。2022 年 1 月 20 日,张爱华写信告知客户保险已投妥,并将保险单与保费账单邮寄给了客户。

外贸业务指引

在国际贸易中,买卖双方处在不同的国家或地区,有的甚至相隔几万公里,所以货物从卖方到买方手中,通常要经过长途运输。在这个过程中,可能会遇到自然灾害或意外事故而使货物遭受各种损失。如果不幸货物全部灭失,损失将相当惨重。为了降低这种风险,可以在货物装运前向保险公司办理货物运输保险,当货物受损时能得到一定的补偿。如果以 CIF 条件成交,在购买保险之前,出口方会根据实际情况,与客户就投保险别及保险金额进行沟通。

一、进口商提出投保要求

发件人(From)	Albert@yaoo.com
收件人(To)	Zhangaihua@mail.hengxin.com
主题(Subject)	Enquiry for Insurance on S/C No. HXEP086

时间(Time)	Dec. 1st, 2021
附件(Attachment)	

Dear Ms. Zhang,

It is pleased to inform you that we have received the S/C No. HXEP086 for 3,600 night lights.

We would be grateful if you will, on our behalf, cover insurance on the goods against F. P. A. and T. P. N. D. for 110% of the invoice value with the People's Insurance Company of China. Moreover, the contract is on a CIF basis, so the insurance premium will be borne by you.

Looking forward to your early reply.

Best regards!

Martin Albert
Purchasing Manager

1. 常用词汇

insurance	保险
cover	给……投保险
F. P. A.	平安险
T. P. N. D.	偷窃、提货不着险
People's Insurance Company of China	中国人民财产保险股份有限公司
premium	保险费

2. 常用句型

(1) We would be grateful if you will, on our behalf, cover insurance on the goods against F. P. A. and T. P. N. D. for 110% of the invoice value with the People's Insurance Company of China.

(2) Moreover, the contract is on a CIF basis, so the insurance premium will be borne by you.

二、与客户沟通保险险别

发件人(From)	Zhangaihua@mail.hengxin.com
收件人(To)	Albert@yaoo.com
主题(Subject)	Re: Enquiry for Insurance on S/C No. HXEP086

时间(Time)	Dec. 2nd, 2021
附件(Attachment)	

Dear Mr. Albert,

I acknowledge receipt of your email of Dec. 1st in which you required insurance to cover T. P. N. D., in addition to F. P. A..

Under normal circumstances, it is unlikely that items such as night lights would be lost or stolen during transit or upon arrival at their destination. Therefore, it is our practice to cover F. P. A. for such commodity. Of course, we can insure the shipment against T. P. N. D. if you require, but the extra premium is at your cost.

Looking forward to your early reply.

Best regards!

Aihua Zhang
Sales Manager
Guangzhou Hengxin Lighting Technology Co., Ltd.
24 Zhannan Road, Yuexiu District, Guangzhou, P. R. China 510010
Email: Zhangaihua@mail.hengxin.com
Tel: 0086-020-86668420
Fax: 0086-020-86668421
Mobile: 13677885566
https://www.hengxin.com

1. 常用词汇

circumstance	条件,情况,环境
practice	通常的做法,惯例
commodity	商品,货物
insure	投保,给……保险
at your cost	费用由你方承担

2. 常用句型

(1) I acknowledge receipt of your email of Dec. 24th in which you required insurance to cover T. P. N. D., in addition to F. P. A..

(2) Under normal circumstances, it is unlikely that items such as night lights would be lost or stolen during transit or upon arrival at their destination.

(3) Therefore, it is our practice to cover F. P. A. for such commodity.

(4) Of course, we can insure the shipment against T. P. N. D. if you require, but the extra premium is at your cost.

营销知识链接

《国际贸易术语解释通则2020》关于CIF卖方投保的规定为：按一般国际贸易惯例，卖方投保的保险金额应按CIF价加成10%；如买卖双方未约定具体险别，则卖方只需投保最低险别。所以，如果客户没有特殊要求，我们按通则的规定投保即可。如果客户提出其他的要求，我们也应该尽量满足，但是额外的费用可以协商由客户支付。

拓展阅读

保险相关常见英文表达

1. 保险相关当事人

保险人　insurer

投保人　insured

受益人　beneficiary

2. 保险金额与保险费

保险金额　insurance amount

保险费　insurance premium

保险费率　insurance premium rate

3. 保险险别——基本险

平安险　free from particular average，F. P. A.

水渍险　with particular average，W. P. A.

一切险　all risks，A. R.

4. 保险险别——附加险

短量险　risk of shortage

偷窃、提货不着险　theft, pilferage and non-delivery，T. P. N. D.

淡水雨淋险　fresh water and/or rain damage，F. W. R. D.

渗漏险　risk of leakage

混杂、沾污险　risk of intermixture and contamination

碰损、破碎险　risk of clash and breakage

串味险　risk of odor

受潮、受热险　damage caused by sweating and heating

锈损险　risk of rust

钩损险　hook damage

包装破裂险　breakage of packing

交货不到险　failure to delivery

进口关税险　import duty risk

舱面险　on deck risk

拒收险　rejection risk
黄曲霉素险　aflatoxin risk
罢工、暴动、民变险　strikes, riots and civil commotions, S.R.C.C.
战争险　war risk
战争险的附加费用险　additional expense-war risk

外贸业务指引

如果以 CIF 条件成交，卖方在购买保险之后，应写信告知客户，并将保险单邮寄给客户，以便遇到保险事故时客户可以据此及时索赔。

三、通知客户保险已投妥

发件人（From）	Zhangaihua@mail.hengxin.com
收件人（To）	Albert@yaoo.com
主题（Subject）	Insurance on Your L/C No. ABL-OP529
时间（Time）	Jan. 20th, 2022
附件（Attachment）	

Dear Mr. Albert,

We are glad to inform you that complying with your request, the shipment has been covered against F.P.A. and T.P.N.D. with PICC for USD 37,323. The policy and our debit note for the extra premium will be forwarded to you by the end of next week.

For your information, we are arranging shipment of 3,600 pieces of night lights you ordered by S.S. "Zhong Shan", sailing on or about the 25th this month.

Best regards!

Aihua Zhang
Sales Manager
Guangzhou Hengxin Lighting Technology Co., Ltd.
24 Zhannan Road, Yuexiu District, Guangzhou, P.R. China 510010
Email：Zhangaihua@mail.hengxin.com
Tel：0086-020-86668420
Fax：0086-020-86668421
Mobile：13677885566
https://www.hengxin.com

1. 常用词汇

policy	保险单
debit note	账单
premium	保险费
forward	发送,寄(商品或信息)
S. S.	轮船(steamship 或 steam ship)
sail	起航

2. 常用句型

(1)We are glad to inform you that complying with your request, the shipment has been covered against F. P. A. and T. P. N. D. with PICC for USD 37,323.

(2)The policy and our debit note for the extra premium will be forwarded to you by the end of next week.

(3)For your information, we are arranging shipment of 3,600 pieces of night lights you ordered by S. S. "Zhong Shan", sailing on or about the 25th this month.

思政园地

(1)培养良好的保险意识,做好保障措施。

跨境贸易涉及的运输距离较远、时间较长,运输存在的风险较大,因此需要做好风险保障,树立正确的保险意识,熟悉各种险别及其承保范围,根据交易业务选择合适的投保险别,采用合适的贸易术语,划分好买卖双方的投保责任,购买运输保险以减少经济损失。

(2)增强工作责任感,提高工作效率。

若我方承担投保责任,则必须及时完成投保手续,以免出现漏保的情况。另外,在对方要求我方办理投保手续的情况下,要将投保条款、投保费用等与对方通过函电沟通清楚并及时将投保情况通知对方。

  课后习题

(一)单项选择

(1)Please insure the goods ( ) A. R. for USD 150,000.
　A. against　　　　B. with　　　　　C. for　　　　　　D. at

(2)As requested, we have covered insurance ( ) 25,000 transistor radios ( ) 10% above the invoice value ( ) All Risks.
　A. on, for, for　　　　　　　　　B. on, for, against
　C. with, for, for　　　　　　　　D. with, for, against

(3)This ( ) is to be covered under our "open-cover" terms.
　A. goods　　　　　　　　　　　　B. consignment
　C. lot　　　　　　　　　　　　　D. insurance

(4) We shall (　　) W. P. A. for you.
　　A. cover　　　　B. arrange　　　　C. provide　　　　D. make

(5) We usually insure (　　) the People's Insurance Company of China for the goods sold on CIF basis.
　　A. for　　　　B. with　　　　C. at　　　　D. in

(6) The extra premium will be (　　) by us.
　　A. bear　　　　B. bears　　　　C. borne　　　　D. bearing

(7) The policy and our debit note for the extra premium will be (　　) to you by the end of next week.
　　A. forward　　　　B. extend　　　　C. forwarded　　　　D. extended

(8) (　　) reply to your enquiry about the insurance on our CIF offers, we wish to give you the following information.
　　A. To　　　　B. In　　　　C. At　　　　D. On

(9) We have insured the shipment against W. P. A. (　　) the rate of 0.3% (　　) the sum of USD 300,000 with PICC.
　　A. at, for　　　　B. at, at　　　　C. for, at　　　　D. for, for

(10) We will cover insurance (　　) your behalf.
　　A. to　　　　B. in　　　　C. at　　　　D. on

(二) 汉译英
(1) 由于我方是按 CIF 订货的，保险应由你方办理。
(2) 我方将按发票金额的 110% 投保此货物。
(3) 我方一般对按 CIF 价出售的货物向中国人民保险公司投保。
(4) 如果你方要求附加险，额外保险费由你方承担。
(5) 在没收到客户具体指示的情况下，我们通常投保水渍险和战争险。

(三) 选择填空
(1) This is to acknowledge receipt of your requesting us to effect (　　) on your order No. 873 concerning 400 cartons of dish washers.

We are pleased to confirm starting to (　　) the above shipment with the People's Insurance Company of China against (　　) for $3,400. The (　　) is being prepared accordingly and will be forwarded to your by the end of the week together with our (　　) for the premium.

For your information, this parcel will be shipped on S/S "Changjiang", sailing on or about the 4th of April.

A. policy

B. insurance

C. debit note

D. cover

E. All Risks

(2) Referring to the Order No. X145 for 1,000 sets of Changhong Brand color TV, you can see that this order was placed on CFR basis.

Now we would like to have the shipment insured (   ). We shall be grateful if you, (   ), kindly arrange to cover the goods against All Risks for 110% of the invoice value, i.e. USD 680,000.

As to the (   ), we will (   ) it to you upon receipt of your debit note, or you may (   ) at sight for the same.

We are looking forward to your speedy reply.

A. on our behalf
B. refund
C. draw on us
D. premium
E. at your end

(四)实训操作

4~5名同学为一组,其中1名同学扮演进口商,其他同学扮演出口商。

扮演出口商的同学结合之前实训操作签订的销售合同,分别撰写一封信函告知进口商保险已投妥。

扮演进口商的同学选出写得最好的一封信并说明原因。

任务四　装运

Task Four: Shipping

任务导入

2022年1月4日,张爱华收到客户来信,对方表示希望我方提前发货,但由于货物不能那么快生产出来,所以张爱华2022年1月5日写信告诉客户无法满足其提前发货的要求。2022年1月25日装船完毕后,张爱华向客户发送了装船通知。

外贸业务指引

我们在备货的同时,要及时与客户沟通、确认具体的装运方式。尽管装运时间、装运港及目的港等信息在合同及信用证中会有明确规定,但在实际操作中往往会因为一些特殊情况导致装运相关事宜发生变化,或者客户会对装运提出新的要求。所以,在出货前,必须和客户详细沟通装运的细节。

一、出口商拒绝提前装运

发件人（From）	Zhangaihua@mail.hengxin.com
收件人（To）	Albert@yaoo.com
主题（Subject）	Earlier Shipment
时间（Time）	Jan. 5th, 2022
附件（Attachment）	

Dear Mr. Albert,

We have received your e-mail of Jan. 4th regarding earlier shipment under L/C No. ABL-OP529.

Upon receipt of your above email, we immediately communicated with the factory. However, the workshop has just informed me that the earliest finish date is Jan. 10th, even though goods have been produced at full speed. Besides, there is no direct container ship from Guangzhou to your port before Jan. 20th.

We are extremely sorry for our inability to advance the shipment. However, we can assure you that we will take special care of your order and will make every effort to catch the earliest shipment date as soon as the goods are ready.

Thanks & Best regards!

Aihua Zhang
Sales Manager
Guangzhou Hengxin Lighting Technology Co., Ltd.
24 Zhannan Road, Yuexiu District, Guangzhou, P. R. China 510010
Email: Zhangaihua@mail.hengxin.com
Tel: 0086-020-86668420
Fax: 0086-020-86668421
Mobile: 13677885566
https://www.hengxin.com

1. 常用词汇

earlier shipment	提前装运
at full speed	全速
container	集装箱，货柜
inability	无能，无力，不能
advance	提前，提早

2. 常用句型

(1)However, the workshop has just informed me that the earliest finish date is Jan. 10th, even though goods have been produced at full speed.

(2)Besides, there is no direct container ship from Guangzhou to your port before Jan. 20th.

(3)We are extremely sorry for our inability to advance the shipment.

(4)However, we can assure you that we will take special care of your order and will make every effort to catch the earliest shipment date as soon as the goods are ready.

二、出口商沟通装运详情

发件人(From)	Zhangaihua@mail.hengxin.com
收件人(To)	Albert@yaoo.com
主题(Subject)	Shipping details for L/C No. ABL-OP529
时间(Time)	Jan. 12nd, 2022
附件(Attachment)	

Dear Mr. Albert,

The goods were completely passed the inspection by ICTI.

I have contacted with forwarder and was advised the cargo cut-off date is Jan. 20th. Due to the upcoming Chinese New Year and the impact of COVID-19, the container is very short and the scheduled sailing date of the 21st has to be postponed to the 25th.

Any progress, I will inform you immediately.

Best regards!

Aihua Zhang
Sales Manager
Guangzhou Hengxin Lighting Technology Co., Ltd.
24 Zhannan Road, Yuexiu District, Guangzhou, P. R. China 510010
Email: Zhangaihua@mail.hengxin.com
Tel: 0086-020-86668420
Fax: 0086-020-86668421
Mobile: 13677885566
https://www.hengxin.com

1. 常用词汇

inspection   检查,检验

forwarder	货运代理
cargo	（船或飞机装载的）货物
cut-off date	截关日
upcoming	即将来临的
scheduled	事先安排的，事先计划的
postpone	推迟
progress	进步，进展，进程

2. 常用句型

(1) I have contacted with forwarder and was advised the cargo cut-off date is Jan. 20th.

(2) Due to the upcoming Chinese New Year and the impact of COVID-19, the container is very short and the scheduled sailing date of the 21st has to be postponed to the 25th.

外贸业务指引

货物装船后，开船前应及时向买方发出装船通知，告知买方货物已出运，并告知客户具体的航次以及预计的到港时间，好让客户了解具体情况，以便其联系目的港的货代，安排货物在当地的清关、运输及其他进口手续等。特别在 CFR 术语项下，向买方发出装船通知尤为重要。若装船通知延误发出导致买方没有及时购买保险，一旦货物发生灭失或损坏，卖方将承担由此造成的损失。

三、出口商发出装船通知

发件人（From）	Zhangaihua@mail.hengxin.com
收件人（To）	Albert@yaoo.com
主题（Subject）	Shipping Advice for L/C No. ABL-OP529
时间（Time）	Jan. 24th, 2022
附件（Attachment）	

Dear Mr. Albert,

We are glad to inform you that the night lights you ordered in November last year under L/C No. ABL-OP529 have been dispatched per S. S. "Zhong Shan" sailing tomorrow (Jan. 25th) from Guangzhou to Bangkok.

We would like you to unpack and examine them immediately upon arrival. Any complaints about damage should be notified to us and the shipping company within ten days.

Meanwhile we've faxed you one set of Shipping Documents covering this consignment which comprise:
1. one copy of non-negotiable Bill of Lading;
2. one copy of Commercial Invoice;

3. one copy of Certificate of Origin；

4. one copy of Certificate of Quality；

5. one copy of Packing List；

6. one copy of Insurance Policy；

7. one copy of Survey Report.

Please confirm your receipt, and we hope this shipment will reach you in time and in good condition to meet with your full satisfaction.

Best regards!

Aihua Zhang
Sales Manager
Guangzhou Hengxin Lighting Technology Co., Ltd.
24 Zhannan Road，Yuexiu District，Guangzhou, P. R. China 510010
Email：Zhangaihua@mail.hengxin.com
Tel：0086-020-86668420
Fax：0086-020-86668421
Mobile：13677885566
https://www.hengxin.com

1. 常用词汇

shipping advice	装船通知
dispatch	发出，发送（邮件、包裹、信息）
unpack	从（箱、包等中）取出
complaint	抱怨，投诉
notify	通报，告知
consignment	装运的货物，运送物
comprise	包含，由……组成
non-negotiable	（文件）不可转让的

2. 常用句型

(1) We are glad to inform you that the night lights you ordered in November last year under L/C No. ABL-OP529 have been dispatched per S. S. "Zhong Shan" sailing tomorrow (Jan. 25th) from Guangzhou to Bangkok.

(2) We would like you to unpack and examine them immediately upon arrival.

(3) Any complaints about damage should be notified to us and the shipping company within ten days.

(4) Meanwhile we've faxed you one set of Shipping Documents covering this consignment which comprise...

(5)Please confirm your receipt, and we hope this shipment will reach you in time and in good condition to meet with your full satisfaction.

外贸业务指引

如果进出口双方以 FOB 术语成交,则由买方负责租船订舱,买卖双方需要就船货衔接的问题进行沟通,以免出现货到船未到或船到货未到的情况,导致产生额外的费用。通常情况下,买方完成租船事宜后,会写信告诉卖方货轮名称、航次、船公司的联系方式等信息。

四、进口商发出装运指示

发件人(From)	Albert@yaoo.com
收件人(To)	Zhangaihua@mail.hengxin.com
主题(Subject)	Shipping Instructions for L/C No. ABL-OP529
时间(Time)	Jan. 15th, 2022
附件(Attachment)	

Dear Ms. Zhang,

Thank you for your email dated Jan. 13rd informing us that the goods will be ready for shipment on Jan. 20th. We have booked shipping space on S.S. "Five Star"(Voyage No. 010F), which is scheduled to sail from HUANGPU on Jan. 22nd.

Please contact Guangdong HuanYu International Freight Forwarding Co., Ltd. for specific arrangements of the shipment. Its contact information is as follows.
Tel:020-37435566
Fax:020-37435567
Address:No. 56, Helong Street, Baiyun District, Guangzhou City

Please send us the shipping advice as soon as the shipment is executed.

Best regards!

Martin Albert
Purchasing Manager

1. 常用词汇

shipping instructions	装运指示
shipping space	舱位
voyage	航行,(尤指)航海,航天

2. 常用句型

(1)We have booked shipping space on S. S. "Five Star"(Voyage No. 010F), which is scheduled to sail from HUANGPU on Jan. 22nd.

(2)Please contact Guangdong HuanYu International Freight Forwarding Co., Ltd. for specific arrangements of the shipment.

外贸业务指引

在处理装运相关事宜时,我们最不愿意遇到的就是延迟交货。但现实往往是复杂多变的,比如碰到了台风等恶劣天气,或工厂产能减少,或因工厂积压订单太多而将订单推迟等等,迫使延迟装运。在这种情况下,需要写信向客户道歉并解释原因,请求客户允许我们延迟交货。

五、出口商请求延迟交货

发件人(From)	Zhangaihua@mail.hengxin.com
收件人(To)	Albert@yaoo.com
主题(Subject)	Postponing Shipment for L/C No. ABL-OP529
时间(Time)	Jan. 25th, 2022
附件(Attachment)	

Dear Mr. Albert,

Sorry to inform you that we have to postpone the shipment of L/C No. ABL-OP529 2-3 weeks later.

We are still in holiday due to coronavirus. In order to effectively control and prevent the epidemic, the government has extended the holiday to Feb. 10th. So please help to give us more time.

Please accept our apology. We will arrange shipment immediately after the holiday.

Best regards!

Aihua Zhang
Sales Manager
Guangzhou Hengxin Lighting Technology Co., Ltd.
24 Zhannan Road, Yuexiu District, Guangzhou, P. R. China 510010
Email: Zhangaihua@mail.hengxin.com
Tel: 0086-020-86668420
Fax: 0086-020-86668421
Mobile: 13677885566
https://www.hengxin.com

1. 常用词汇

coronavirus	冠状病毒
epidemic	流行病
apology	歉意

2. 常用句型

(1)Sorry to inform you that we have to postpone the shipment of L/C No. ABL-OP529 2-3 weeks later.

(2)So please help to give us more time.

思政园地

(1)树立良好的时间观念,坚守契约精神。

要树立良好的时间观念。作为出口商要注意在约定日期前完成装运发货,作为进口商要及时跟踪对方的发货情况。坚守契约精神,按照合同约定完成装运任务,买卖双方及时沟通、相互配合,履行好合同义务。

(2)培养爱岗敬业、忠于职守的精神。

为了准时完成装运任务,必要时需要多班轮流、全力生产,因此要培养爱岗敬业、忠于职守的精神,在保质保量的前提下完成装运发货工作。同时,要及时将装运情况通过函电通知客户,让客户感受到我方对该业务的重视和对工作的热情,向其展示我方是值得信赖的合作伙伴。

课后习题

(一)单项选择

(1)Please effect insurance (　　) the cargo for RMB 12,000, by S.S. "Wind".
A. by　　　　　B. at　　　　　C. with　　　　　D. on

(2)We have shipped today by the S.S. "Dong Feng" (　　) to leave tomorrow.
A. scheduled　　B. made　　　C. planned　　　D. decided

(3)Please make the shipment during June/July (　　) two equal (　　).
A. of...lot　　B. in...lots　　C. of...lots　　D. in...lot

(4)We will make every (　　) to ship the goods as early as possible, and we feel (　　) that the shipment will be satisfactory to you in every respect.
A. effect, sure　　B. effort, sure　　C. effect, assure　　D. effort, assure

(5)Sometimes, transshipment and partial shipment are (　　) by the buyer.
A. permission　　B. permitting　　C. prohibited　　D. prohibiting

(6)We wish to receive your shipping advice soon for the goods under the captioned (　　).
A. letter　　　B. cable　　　C. contract　　　D. communication

(7)The workshop has just informed me that the earliest finish date is Jan. 10th, (　　) goods have been produced at full speed.

A. in case to　　　　B. but　　　　　C. even though　　　D. because

(8) The goods have been dispatched per S. S. "Zhong Shan" (　　) tomorrow (Jan. 25th) from Guangzhou to Bangkok.

A. sail　　　　　　B. sailing　　　　C. sailed　　　　　D. sails

(9) We would like you to (　　) and examine them immediately upon arrival.

A. unpack　　　　　B. unpacked　　　C. pack　　　　　　D. packed

(10) We have booked shipping space on S. S. "Five Star", which is (　　) to sail from HUANGPU on Jan. 22nd.

A. schedule　　　　B. schedules　　　C. scheduling　　　D. scheduled

(二)汉译英

(1)123号合同项下的货物已经备妥待运。

(2)我们急需此货,恳请你方提前发运。

(3)请注意,货物须装于"麻雀"号货轮。该货轮预计1月4日到达上海。请确认货物能及时到达码头待运。

(4)兹告知你方347号订单项下的货物已经装于"月亮河"号货轮,航次:443EO。此货轮将于5月15日离港,预计30天内到达你方口岸。

(5)按你方要求,兹随函附寄一整套的装船单据,包括商业发票、装箱单和已装船清洁提单。所有单据均一式三份。

(三)选择填空

(1) We have already received your email of Feb. 25th. We feel sorry for the (　　), which was caused by the unexpected late arrival of the goods from the place of origin. It is our fault not letting you know the cause in time.

In addition, because of the (　　), the harbor is now icebound and not navigable. After communication with related officials, we now have settled the shipment time.

The shipment of 30 tons Linseeds under S/C No. 253 will be arranged to go forth (　　) S. S. "JianAn". The ship will (　　) Tianjin on or about March 5. We will email you immediately when the ship (　　).

Thanks for your understanding and cooperation.

A. sets off

B. shipment delay

C. terrible weather

D. sail from

E. on board

(2) We are pleased to inform you that the 5,000 dozen silk pajamas under your L/C No. KP234 have now been (　　) via "Victory" from Ningbo, due to arrive at Hamburg on August 11, 2010.

(　　) of the relative shipping (　　) were sent to you by courier service, ensuring that you can take (　　) of the goods on their arrival at your designated port.

We hope this shipment will reach you on time and the goods contained satisfy your (   ).

    A. Copies

    B. specifications

    C. possession

    D. documents

    E. dispatched

(四)实训操作

4~5名同学为一组,其中1名同学扮演进口商,其他同学扮演出口商。

扮演出口商的同学结合之前实训操作中信用证的要求,撰写一封装船通知。

扮演进口商的同学选出写得最好的一封装船通知并说明原因。

项目五　客户服务

Project Five: Customer Service

学习目标

【思政目标】

培养科学的思维方法；
培养良好的同理心和共情力；
培养以人为本的服务意识，增强责任担当；
培养辩证思维和创新能力。

【知识目标】

掌握索赔、理赔及维护老客户相关的常用英文词汇及句型；
掌握处理客户索赔和维护老客户相关信函的内容和写作方法；
掌握处理客户索赔的技巧和方法；
掌握维护老客户的技巧和方法。

【能力目标】

能够熟练阅读索赔函；
能够正确处理客户的索赔并撰写理赔函；
能够撰写维护老客户的相关信函。

任务一 索赔与理赔

Task One: Claim and Settlement

任务导入

客户收到产品后,发现其中3箱货物损毁,于2022年2月5日写信给张爱华进行索赔。收到索赔函之后,张爱华立刻回信给客户表达歉意并承诺立刻展开调查。调查结果出来后,张爱华于2022年2月8日写信向客户详细说明相关情况,并提出理赔方案。之后,张爱华就理赔的方式和理赔的金额与客户进行了谈判沟通,并确定了最终方案。

外贸业务指引

在进出口贸易中,由于各种因素的影响,不履行或不完全按照合同规定履行合同的情况经常发生,较为常见的是买方就质量、数量、包装或交货问题向卖方投诉或索赔。所谓索赔,是指遭受损害的一方在争议发生后,根据合同或法律的有关规定,向违约方提出赔偿要求。

一、索赔函

发件人(From)	Albert@yaoo.com
收件人(To)	Zhangaihua@mail.hengxin.com
主题(Subject)	Quality Claim-IMPORTANT!!!
时间(Time)	Feb. 5th, 2022
附件(Attachment)	Photos and List of Damaged Goods

Dear Ms. Zhang,

We received the goods under L/C No. ABL-OP529 this morning. Unfortunately, three cartons of the goods are seriously damaged, and 100 pieces of night lights are dirty and cracked. Therefore, we would like to file a claim for the 100 pieces of damaged night lights.

Attached are photos and a list of the damaged packing and goods. We look forward to your early response and settlement.

Best regards!

Martin Albert

Purchasing Manager

1. 常用词汇

claim	索赔
damage	损坏，损害
cracked	破裂的，有裂纹的
file	提起（诉讼），提出（申请）
settlement	赔付，偿付

2. 常用句型

(1) Unfortunately, three cartons of the goods are seriously damaged, and 100 pieces of night lights are dirty and cracked.

(2) Therefore, we would like to file a claim for the 100 pieces of damaged night lights.

外贸业务指引

在外贸实务中，收到客户投诉是经常的事，投诉包括品质问题、服务问题、交货期问题等，需要我们在第一时间处理并给出答复。尤其是品质问题的投诉，往往是最重要也是最伤感情的，一旦处理不好，就会影响到与客户未来的合作，必须慎之又慎。

二、理赔函

发件人(From)	Zhangaihua@mail.hengxin.com
收件人(To)	Albert@yaoo.com
主题(Subject)	Re: Quality Claim-IMPORTANT!!!
时间(Time)	Feb. 6th, 2022
附件(Attachment)	

Dear Mr. Albert,

We are sorry to learn from your email dated Feb. 5th that 100 pieces of night lights have been so damaged as to be unsaleable.

We shall immediately make a thorough investigation, but this will take about two days. We will notify you of the result upon completion of the investigation. If we are at fault, the compensation will be made at once.

> We apologize for any inconvenience we have caused.
>
> Best regards!
>
> Aihua Zhang
> Sales Manager
> Guangzhou Hengxin Lighting Technology Co., Ltd.
> 24 Zhannan Road, Yuexiu District, Guangzhou, P. R. China 510010
> Email: Zhangaihua@mail.hengxin.com
> Tel: 0086-020-86668420
> Fax: 0086-020-86668421
> Mobile: 13677885566
> https://www.hengxin.com

1. 常用词汇

thorough	彻底的,完全的,深入的,细致的
investigation	（正式的）调查,侦查
completion	完成,结束
fault	责任,过错,过失
compensation	赔偿金,赔偿
apologize	道歉

2. 常用句型

(1) We shall immediately make a thorough investigation, but this will take about two days.

(2) We will notify you of the result upon completion of the investigation.

(3) If we are at fault, the compensation will be made at once.

(4) We apologize for any inconvenience we have caused.

营销知识链接

处理客户的投诉和索赔时，首先态度要好，一开始客户正在气头上，我们要尽可能安抚客户的情绪。所以，第一时间回信给客户并提供解决方案非常重要。如果事情比较复杂，需要时间来调查，也应该立刻回信给客户，说明大概需要几天时间来调查，并在调查结果出来后及时告知客户，并提出解决方案。

外贸业务指引

如果调查结果证明不是我方的责任，在写信告知客户时要随函附上相关证据。有时客户态度可能不是太好，我们也尽量不要与客户产生争执，而是应该积极帮助客户想办法来解决问题。只有学会体谅客户，能够换位思考，才能保证客户即使遭遇了这次的不愉快，以后仍然会继续和我们合作。

三、理赔函——拒绝赔偿

发件人（From）	Zhangaihua@mail.hengxin.com
收件人（To）	Albert@yaoo.com
主题（Subject）	Re：Quality Claim-IMPORTANT！！！
时间（Time）	Feb. 8th，2022
附件（Attachment）	

Dear Mr. Albert，

We have looked into all of our records related to this business，and as far as we can find，the goods in question were in good condition when they left here，as evidenced by the Bill of Lading. Therefore，it is quite obvious that the damage complained of must have occurred in transit.

In this situation，we are apparently not responsible for the damage and would suggest you lodge a claim on the shipping company who should be held responsible. We would be glad to take the matter up on your behalf with the shipping company concerned if you require.

Best regards！

Aihua Zhang
Sales Manager
Guangzhou Hengxin Lighting Technology Co.，Ltd.
24 Zhannan Road，Yuexiu District，Guangzhou，P. R. China 510010
Email：Zhangaihua@mail.hengxin.com
Tel：0086-020-86668420
Fax：0086-020-86668421
Mobile：13677885566
https://www.hengxin.com

1. 常用词汇

look into	调查
so far as	就……而言
evidence	证实,证明
occur	发生
apparently	看来,显然
responsible	有责任的,负责的,承担义务的

lodge	正式提出（投诉、抗议、指控、要求）
on your behalf	代表你方
concerned	相关的

2. 常用句型

（1）We have looked into all of our records related to this business, and as far as we can find, the goods in question were in good condition when they left here, as evidenced by the Bill of Lading.

（2）Therefore, it is quite obvious that the damage complained of must have occurred in transit.

（3）In this situation, we are apparently not responsible for the damage and would suggest you lodge a claim on the shipping company who should be held responsible.

（4）We would be glad to take the matter up on your behalf with the shipping company concerned if you require.

外贸业务指引

如果调查出来确实是我方的责任，我们不仅需要在第一时间向客户道歉，还需要仔细研究调查结果并给出解决方案，而不是一句简单的道歉了事，因为这对客户来说很不礼貌，也是相当不负责任的。要站在客户的角度换位思考，如果这个问题发生了，客户能够怎么办？应该怎么做才能尽快帮他解决困难？有什么应对的办法？

四、理赔函——道歉并提供解决方案

发件人(From)	Zhangaihua@mail.hengxin.com
收件人(To)	Albert@yaoo.com
主题(Subject)	Re：Quality Claim-IMPORTANT!!!
时间(Time)	Feb. 8th, 2022
附件(Attachment)	

Dear Mr. Albert,

Regarding your claim about damaged night lights, we have investigated the matter in detail and discovered that some of the night lights cracked because of the too high temperature during processing.

In order not to affect the cooperation between us, we have decided to immediately send replacements to you of which the quality is guaranteed to be all right. In addition, we will give you 20 pieces of our new products worth USD 20 each as compensation for your trial sales. Meanwhile, we have taken some corrective measures to prevent a repetition of the same in the future.

Please accept our apologies for the trouble caused to you.

Best regards!

Aihua Zhang

Sales Manager

Guangzhou Hengxin Lighting Technology Co., Ltd.

24 Zhannan Road, Yuexiu District, Guangzhou, P. R. China 510010

Email：Zhangaihua@mail.hengxin.com

Tel：0086-020-86668420

Fax：0086-020-86668421

Mobile：13677885566

https://www.hengxin.com

1. 常用词汇

process	加工，处理
replacement	替代品，替换物
guarantee	保证，担保
compensation	赔偿金，补偿金
trial sales	试销
corrective	纠正的，矫正的
repetition	重复，重说，重做

2. 常用句型

(1) Regarding your claim about damaged night lights, we have investigated the matter in detail and discovered that some of the night lights cracked because of the too high temperature during processing.

(2) In order not to affect the cooperation between us, we have decided to immediately send replacements to you of which the quality is guaranteed to be all right.

(3) In addition, we will give you 20 pieces of our new products worth USD 20 each as compensation for your trial sales.

(4) Meanwhile, we have taken some corrective measures to prevent a repetition of the same in the future.

外贸业务指引

在处理客户索赔时，往往会面临一个比较难以解决的问题，就是赔款的金额问题。具体赔多少？怎么赔？如果客户索赔的金额太大怎么办？这都是我们业务员需要认真考虑的。不是一味让步，或是一味强硬就可以解决问题。谈判需要技巧，需要减少彼此的损失，为未来的合作铺平道路。

五、理赔函——商量赔款金额

发件人(From)	Zhangaihua@mail.hengxin.com
收件人(To)	Albert@yaoo.com
主题(Subject)	Re：Quality Claim-IMPORTANT！！！
时间(Time)	Feb. 10th，2022
附件(Attachment)	

Dear Mr. Albert，

I have discussed with my manager about the compensation. I'm regretful we couldn't accept the compensation up to USD 8,000，because the total value of the damaged night lights is only USD 1,660.

Please help to find our two suggestions as follows：

1. We will make you a compensation of USD 1,800 by the way of T/T. In future orders this year，we could keep the price and give you an extra 2％ discount as compensation.

2. We'll ship replacements of the damaged night lights at once and give you USD 500 as compensation.

Please give me your comment soon.

Best regards！

Aihua Zhang
Sales Manager
Guangzhou Hengxin Lighting Technology Co.，Ltd.
24 Zhannan Road，Yuexiu District，Guangzhou，P. R. China 510010
Email：Zhangaihua@mail.hengxin.com
Tel：0086-020-86668420
Fax：0086-020-86668421
Mobile：13677885566
https://www.hengxin.com

1. 常用词汇

suggestion　　　　　　　　　　建议，提议
at once　　　　　　　　　　　立刻，马上

2. 常用句型

(1) I'm regretful we couldn't accept the compensation up to USD 8,000，because the

total value of the damaged night lights is only USD 1,660.

(2) In future orders this year, we could keep the price and give you an extra 2% discount as compensation.

(3) We'll ship replacements of the damaged night lights at once and give you USD 500 as compensation.

营销知识链接

客户的索赔不一定都要用钱来解决,也可以给客户重新补发一批货,或者发一些其他的产品让客户免费试销,还可以在下次合作时给客户打个折。如果直接用钱一次性赔付,客户拿到赔款后,很有可能再也不会与我们合作。所以我们还要尽可能想办法维系住与客户的关系,用未来给予折扣的方式吸引客户就是一个不错的办法。如果赔款金额比较大,还可以与客户商量分期赔付,这样也能够争取与客户进一步沟通的机会,以便再次取得客户的信任。

思政园地

(1) 培养科学思维方法,以理性思维解决问题。

在索赔与理赔环节,情绪问题容易伤害买卖双方的和气,导致纠纷问题更加严重。因此,不能让恶劣情绪冲昏头脑,应该时刻保持头脑清晰,培养科学思维方法并以理性思维解决问题。若我方为主动索赔方,应详细向对方阐明情况并寻求解决问题的合理方式。同时,函电沟通中要以礼貌、包容的态度促使双方互相配合并顺利解决纠纷。

(2) 培养良好的同理心和共情力。

良好的同理心和共情力更能展现我方为客户利益着想的处事态度。若我方为失误的一方,应及时向客户表达歉意,并给出合理的解决方案,转危为机,重新争取客户的信任与未来合作的机会;若我方为无责任方,出于友好往来的目的,也应对客户的遭遇表达惋惜之情,并帮助对方解决问题。

课后习题

(一) 单项选择

(1) We are sorry for our mistake in the number, ( ) resulted ( ) you receiving the wrong goods.

  A. that, of   B. this, from   C. which, in   D. it, is

(2) You can file a claim with the insurance company in your area, which will ( ) the loss incurred.

  A. compensate   B. compensate for

  C. compensate to you   D. compensate you

(3) The goods under Contract No. AM516 left here ( ).

  A. in a good condition   B. in good conditions

  C. in good condition   D. in the good condition

(4)We think the best procedure will be to (　　) by an expert, and we are arranging for this to be done.

　　A. have examined the pieces　　　　B. have the pieces examined
　　C. examine the pieces　　　　　　　D. have the pieces examination

(5)It would help us a treat deal if you could (　　) the shipment from August to July.

　　A. presence　　B. advantage　　　C. advance　　　D. effect

(6)Please be informed that we will(　　) shipment of the second lot within 15 days of dispatch of the first lot.

　　A. affect　　　B. effect　　　C. effort　　　D. select

(7)We hope no difficulty will (　　) in connection with the insurance claim and thank you in advance for your trouble on our behalf.

　　A. rise　　　B. raise　　　C. arise　　　D. arouse

(8)It is most essential that the delivery (　　) punctual, otherwise our summer sale can not be carried out.

　　A. will be　　B. would be　　C. has been　　D. should be

(9)Case No. 12 was found to be 4 packages (　　).

　　A. too short　　B. shortage　　C. to shorten　　D. short

(10)Any complaint about the quality of products should be (　　) within 15 days after their arrival.

　　A. lodged　　B. put　　　C. found　　　D. propose

(二)汉译英

(1)调查表明,货物的损坏系包装不良所致。

(2)因为短重我们要向你方就这批货索赔,金额为3200美元。

(3)我们很抱歉不能接受你方索赔,因为箱子离开此地时完好无损,损坏显然发生在运输途中。

(4)请将所有货物退还,我们将请船运公司来检查损失,以便他们安排赔偿。

(5)我方对此事带来的不便深表歉意,并保证采取一切措施避免此类差错再次发生。

(三)选择填空

(1)We have received the Porcelains under Order No. 123. Your prompt delivery is much appreciated.

However, when we unpack the goods, we find that the porcelains in Case No. 3 are completely (　　) and thus are (　　).

After (　　), we find the breakage is due to improper packing, and you should be responsible for the loss we suffer from it. Therefore, we would like to register a (　　) with you for USD 3,000 as well as the inspection fee.

We now enclose the(　　) and the debit note for your reference and expect an early settlement to this matter.

A. claim

B. broken

C. inspection certificate

D. unsalable

E. investigation

(2) Your letter of Sep. 21st, 2022 has been received. We are sorry to learn that 3 cases of the porcelains are broken due to (　　).

Recently we have received so many orders from Europe that we are (　　), which leads to mistakes in packing. We feel sorry for the inconvenience you have suffered from that.

We would be obliged if you could send back the broken porcelains by the earliest steamer available (　　). We have sent you a (　　) of the porcelains and the relative documents will be mailed as soon as they are ready.

We hope that you will be satisfied with what we have done to this (　　).

A. replacement

B. improper package

C. accident

D. short-handed

E. at our expense

(四)实训操作

4~5名同学为一组,其中1名同学扮演进口商,其他同学扮演出口商。

假设货物到达目的港后,进口商发现少了三箱货物,扮演进口商的同学结合之前实训操作中的产品相关信息,撰写一封索赔函。

扮演出口商的同学针对进口商的索赔函,分别撰写理赔函。

扮演进口商的同学选出写得最好的一封理赔函并说明原因。

任务二　售后跟进

Task Two: After-sale Follow-up

任务导入

处理完客户的索赔后,该笔业务终于告一段落了。但张爱华并没有放松下来,为了维护好Albert先生这位客户,2022年5月5日,张爱华写信给客户,询问这批产品在泰国本地的销售情况,以及他们对产品的看法和建议。2022年6月1日,公司推出新产品后,张爱华又写信向客户推荐该新产品,寻求再次合作的机会。

外贸业务指引

产品销售给客户以后,我们不能就不管不问了,而是应该跟进了解客户的销售情况(或使用情况)。比如:产品在当地的销量如何?消费者的评价如何?有哪些地方需要改进?跟市场上同类产品相比有什么优缺点?价格上是不是有足够的竞争力?这些都需要和客户沟通讨论,为未来的产品生产、改进及销售提供参考。

一、询问产品销售情况

发件人(From)	Zhangaihua@mail.hengxin.com
收件人(To)	Albert@yaoo.com
主题(Subject)	Feedback on Market Acceptance
时间(Time)	May. 5th, 2022
附件(Attachment)	

Dear Mr. Albert,

Much thanks for your purchase of 3,600 pieces of night lights three months ago.

We would very appreciate if you could give us feedback on market acceptance as competition is getting stronger. We'd like to know customers' thinking and feelings about our products, as well as the strengths and weaknesses of our products compared to those of our competitors.

We will improve our designs and patterns based on the information you provide to make customers more satisfactory, promote the sales and achieve a win-win situation. By the way, do you have some new purchasing plans?

Looking forward to your reply.

Best regards!

Aihua Zhang
Sales Manager
Guangzhou Hengxin Lighting Technology Co., Ltd.
24 Zhannan Road, Yuexiu District, Guangzhou, P. R. China 510010
Email: Zhangaihua@mail.hengxin.com
Tel: 0086-020-86668420
Fax: 0086-020-86668421
Mobile: 13677885566
https://www.hengxin.com

1. 常用词汇

feedback   反馈的意见(或信息)

competition	竞争
strength	优势，优点，长处
weakness	劣势，弱点
compare	比较，对比
pattern	图案，花样，式样
win-win	对各方都有益的，双赢的

2. 常用句型

(1) We would very appreciate if you could give us feedback on market acceptance as competition is getting stronger.

(2) We'd like to know customers' thinking and feelings about our products, as well as the strengths and weaknesses of our products compared to those of our competitors.

(3) We will improve our designs and patterns based on the information you provide to make customers more satisfactory, promote the sales and achieve a win-win situation.

外贸业务指引

如果我们的产品更新换代，或者有新产品上市，应该第一时间通知老客户，以便他们预留足够的时间来开发新客户，或者及时调整市场策略。无论是信息延迟或滞后，让客户没有及时做好准备，还是有新产品冲击客户所在地的本土市场，致使其原有的库存压力增大，都容易让客户在资金和销售上出现问题，处于被动的境地。

二、向客户推荐新产品

发件人（From）	Zhangaihua@mail.hengxin.com
收件人（To）	Albert@yaoo.com
主题（Subject）	New Products / Night Lights / Promotion
时间（Time）	Jun. 1st, 2022
附件（Attachment）	

Dear Mr. Albert,

We are so pleased that you chose a series of our products in your purchase order four months ago. I am confident that our friendship and cooperation will be further intensified as time goes by.

Last week, the R&D Department has updated our online catalogue on our official website, which covers the latest products in stock. We believe that you will find some of our new designs most fashionable in the market, especially the night lights. We are planning a promotion in Thailand this month, please take advantage of this opportunity to get your orders.

Looking forward to your early reply.

Best regards!

Aihua Zhang
Sales Manager
Guangzhou Hengxin Lighting Technology Co., Ltd.
24 Zhannan Road, Yuexiu District, Guangzhou, P. R. China 510010
Email：Zhangaihua@mail.hengxin.com
Tel：0086-020-86668420
Fax：0086-020-86668421
Mobile：13677885566
https://www.hengxin.com

1. 常用词汇

series	一连串，一系列
confident	有信心的
intensify	加强，强化
go by	时间流逝
R&D Department	研发部门

2. 常用句型

(1) Last week, the R&D Department has updated our online catalogue on our official website, which covers the latest products in stock.

(2) We believe that you will find some of our new designs most fashionable in the market, especially the night lights.

(3) We are planning a promotion in Thailand this month, please take advantage of this opportunity to get your orders.

思政园地

(1) 树立以人为本的服务意识，增强责任担当。

及时了解客户的销售情况、消费者的使用情况，从客户利益出发，为客户提供更高水平、更全面的服务内容。对售后出现的问题，应该及时与客户做好函电沟通并合理解决。良好的售后服务和售后保障，能更好地彰显产品过硬的质量水平，促使与客户的关系走得更长远、更稳固。

(2) 提高辩证思维能力，发挥不断创新的精神。

增强辩证思维能力，提高驾驭复杂局面、处理复杂问题的本领。虚心接受客户的评价反馈，及时发现问题、分析问题、解决问题，以便更好地改善产品和服务水平。从售后跟进中发挥创新精神，以灵活有效的方式维系好与客户之间的关系。

课后习题

(一)单项选择

(1) What they sometimes lack is (　　) from the people who they hope will use their products.
　　A. demand　　　　B. require　　　　C. feedback　　　　D. claim

(2) We'd like to know the strengths and weaknesses of our products (　　) to those of our competitors.
　　A. compare　　　B. compares　　　C. compared　　　D. comparing

(3) We will improve our designs and patterns (　　) the information you provide.
　　A. based in　　　B. based on　　　C. basing in　　　D. basing on

(4) If the item is not (　　), you will get your money back.
　　A. satisfy　　　B. satisfied　　　C. satisfactory　　　D. satisfaction

(5) We would very appreciate (　　) you could give me feedback on market acceptance (　　) competition is getting stronger.
　　A. because, as　　B. if, as　　C. because, if　　D. as, if

(6) I am (　　) that our business will go further.
　　A. believe　　　B. believable　　　C. confident　　　D. confidence

(7) The catalogue covers the (　　) products in stock.
　　A. last　　　B. latest　　　C. late　　　D. later

(8) Our friendship and cooperation will be further intensified (　　) time goes by.
　　A. as　　　B. since　　　C. due to　　　D. if

(9) We are (　　) a promotion in Thailand this month.
　　A. plan　　　B. planned　　　C. planning　　　D. plans

(10) Please (　　) this opportunity to get your orders.
　　A. take advantage of　　　　　　B. to your advantage
　　C. to good advantage　　　　　　D. advantage

(二)汉译英

(1) 如果您能告诉我们当地市场的销售情况,我们将非常感激。
(2) 我们想了解客户对我们产品的想法和感受。
(3) 我们会根据你方提供的信息改进我们的设计和式样,以更好地满足你方的需求,促进销售,实现共赢。
(4) 相信您会发现我们的一些新设计在市场上很流行,尤其是夜灯。
(5) 我们计划这个月在泰国进行促销活动,请抓住这个机会下订单。

(三)选择填空

(1) Please allow me to introduce our (　　) product, silicon cover set for mobile device. They are produced (　　) iPhone / iTouch & iPad. (　　), these accessories have done well in US market. Do you have some idea for the hot-selling models in auto and DIY field? I'm

going to the US next week, not only for (   ) the Las Vegas fair, but for visiting the **BESTBUY, HOME DEPOT**, and **WAL-MART** to find some interesting items as well. And I hope to see you then to discuss for our (   ). I have interest to develop some new products for the US & Canadian market.

A. attending

B. new series of

C. for

D. future projects

E. As I know

(2) Sorry to trouble you at the moment. I would like to (   ) you about your last order for 56 pcs CRV screwdriver bits kit. Have you sold them (   )? Now we developed a similar set, and used carbon steel, instead. The pricing could be roughly 30% (   ). We plan to do a (   ) in Holland this June. Do you have (   ) this set?

A. lower

B. promotion

C. check with

D. interest in

E. out

(四)实训操作

4～5 名同学为一组,其中 1 名同学扮演进口商,其他同学扮演出口商。

扮演出口商的同学结合之前实训操作中的相关信息,撰写一封询问产品销售情况的信函。

扮演进口商的同学选出写得最好的一封信函并说明原因。

参考文献

[1] 毅冰.十天搞定外贸函电[M].北京:中国海关出版社,2012.
[2] 周道.外贸英语函电[M].北京:对外经济贸易大学出版社,2015.
[3] 伊辉春.新编外贸英语函电[M].北京:化学工业出版社,2016.
[4] 徐俊.外贸英语函电实务[M].北京:中国商业出版社,2016.
[5] 王珍.外贸英语函电[M].2版.大连:大连理工大学出版社,2018.
[6] 张颖,张键.外贸英文函电[M].北京:电子工业出版社,2018.
[7] 王黎明.外贸英语函电[M].4版.北京:机械工业出版社,2022.
[8] 李艳丽.外贸英语函电[M].济南:山东人民出版社,2010.
[9] 福步(FOB)外贸论坛:http://bbs.fobshanghai.com/index.php.
[10] JAC外贸实战:https://www.chinajac.com.